I am grateful to God for everything! And I believe that the meaning of life is to make sense of other lives.

Édna Lessa

2024

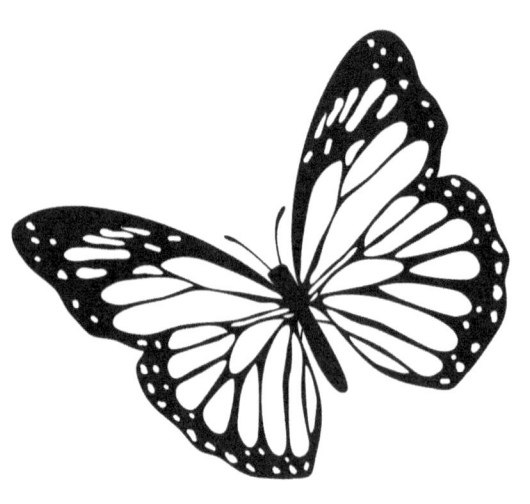
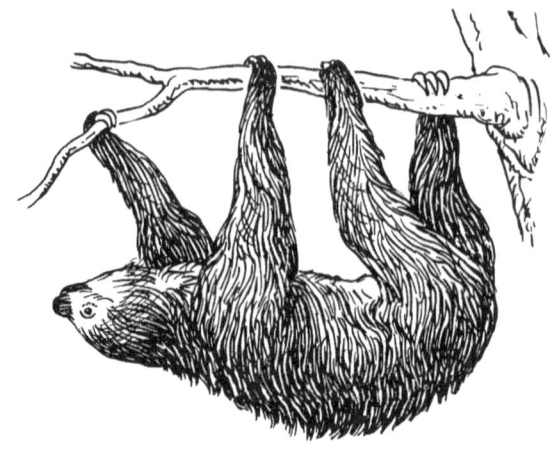

This Book Belongs to:

○———————————————————○

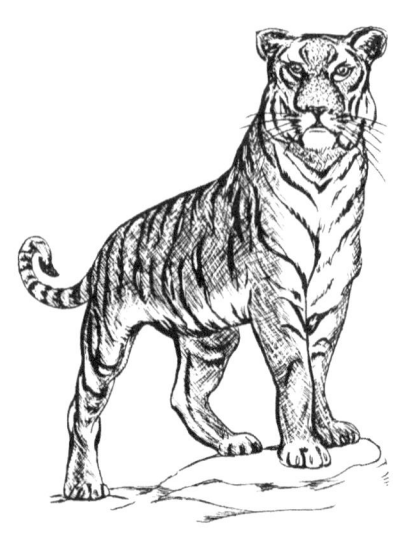
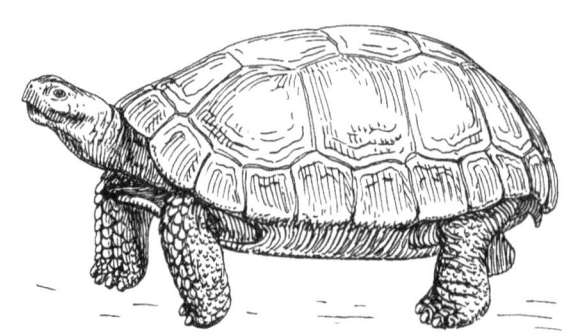

E.L.©
all rights reserved

ALL RIGHTS RESERVED©
2024

No part of this publication may be reproduced, distributed, or transmitted in any form or by any means, including photocopying, recording, or other electronic or mechanical methods, without the prior written permission of the publisher, except for brief quotations incorporated in critical reviews and other specific noncommercial uses. Any unauthorized replica of this work is prohibited.

E.L.©
Edna's Lessa publications

Test Color Page

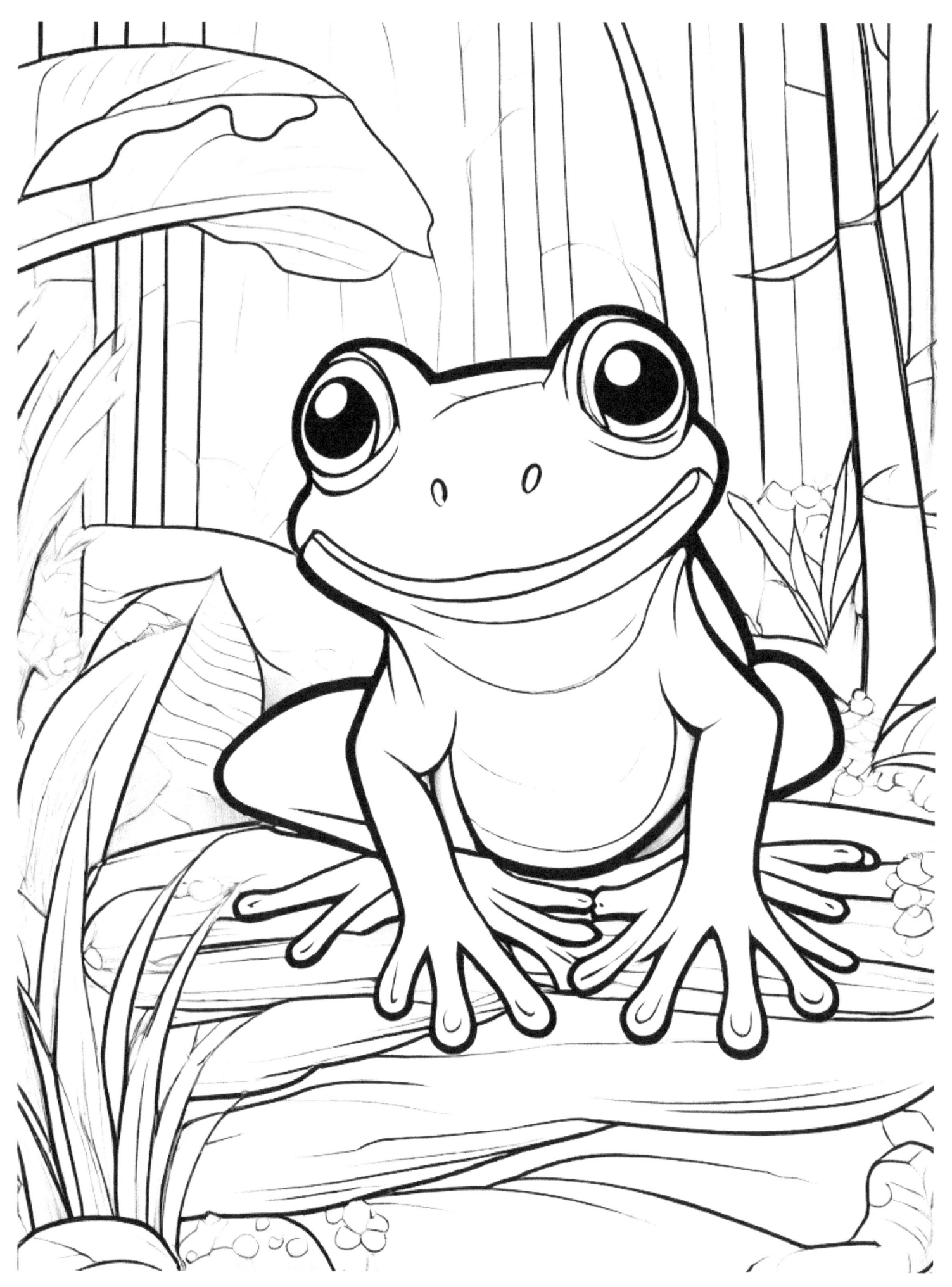

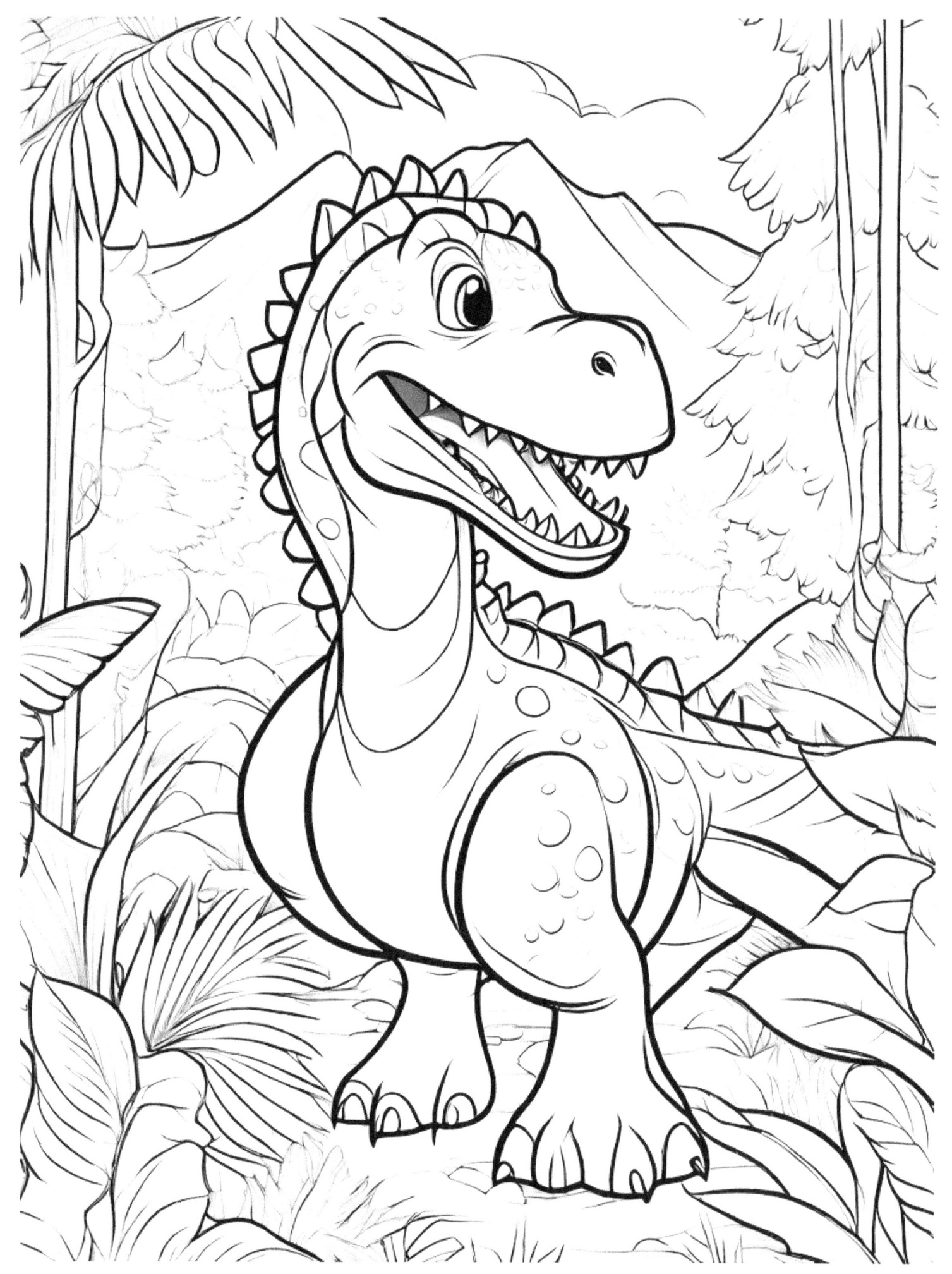

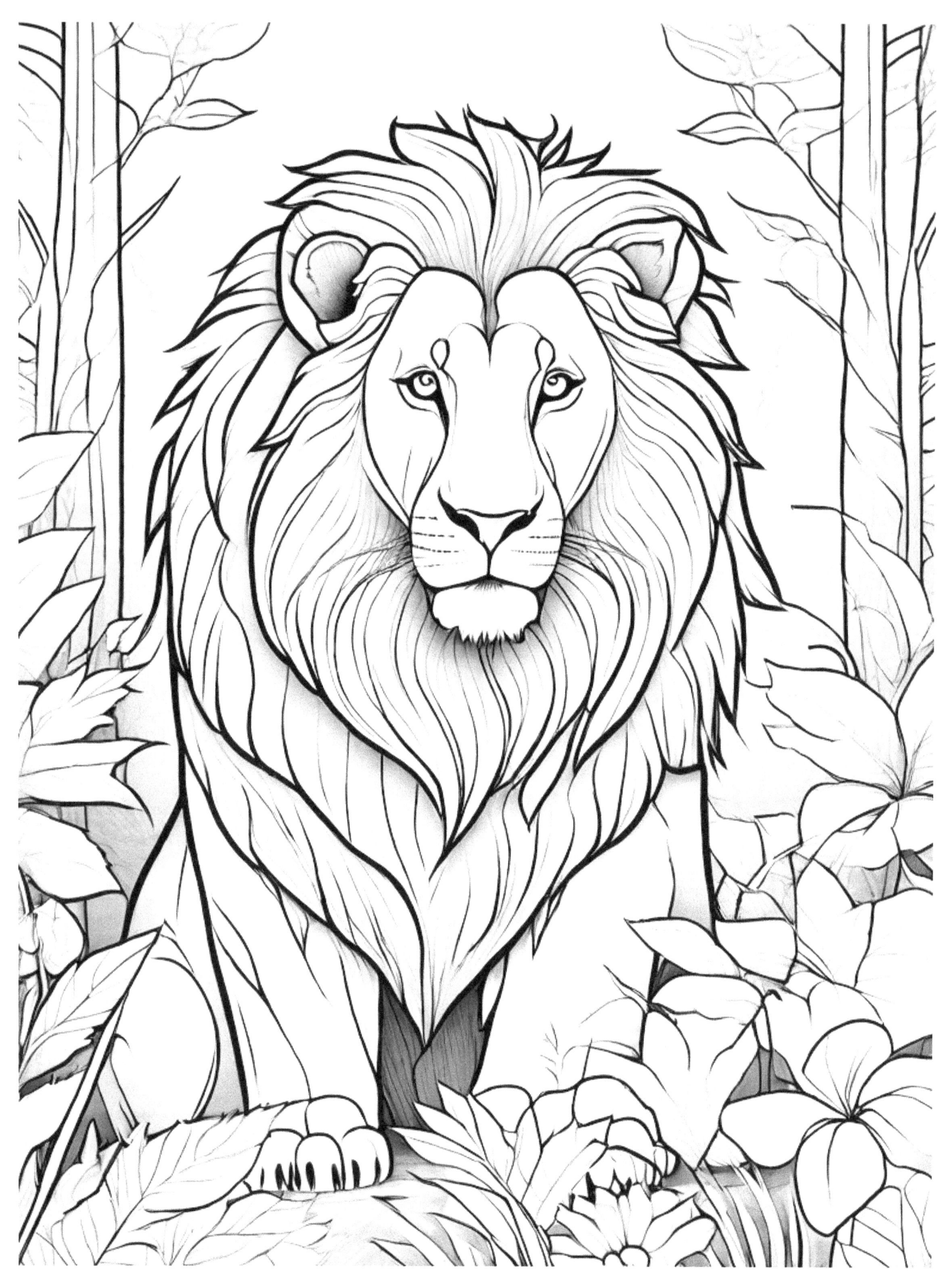

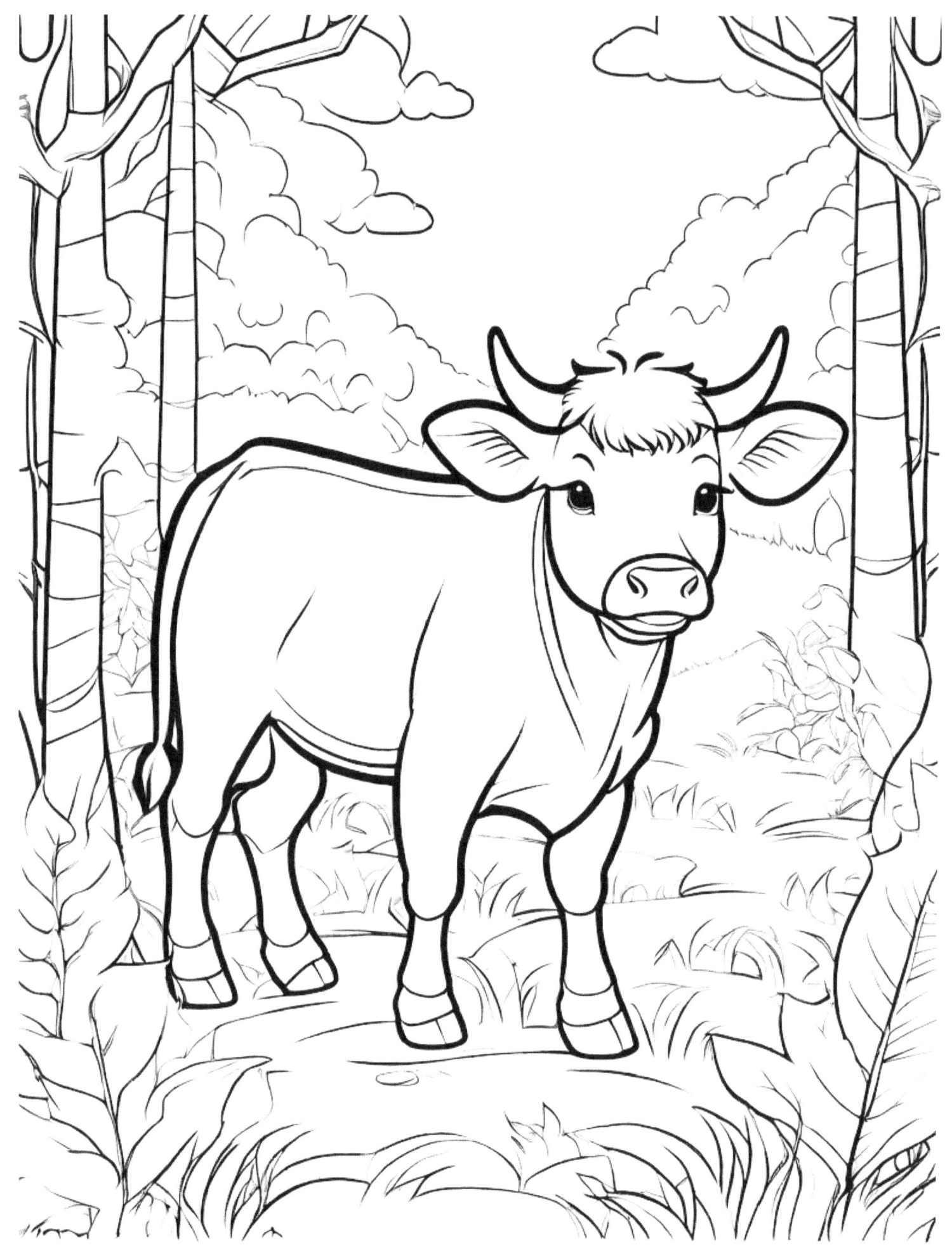

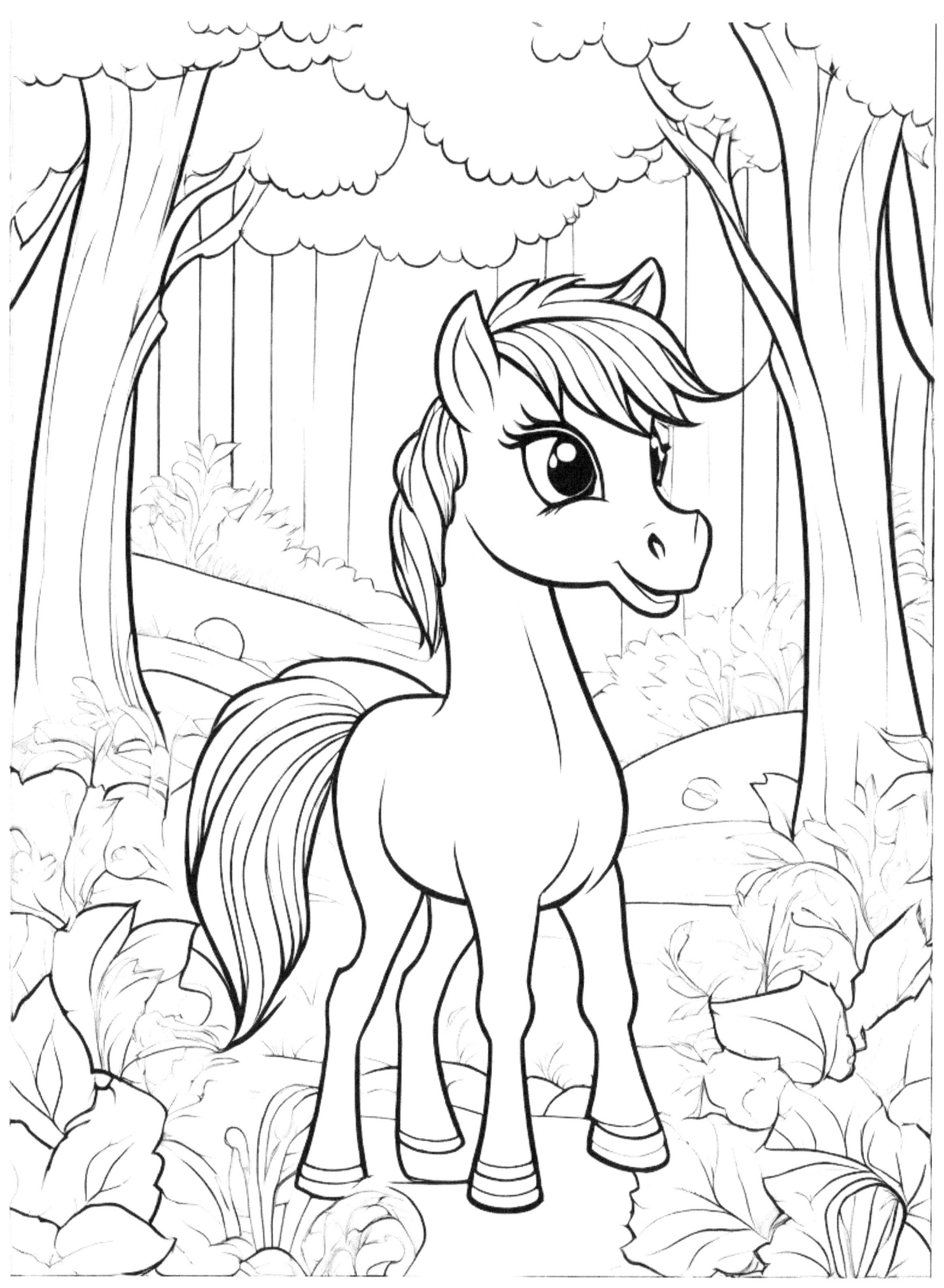

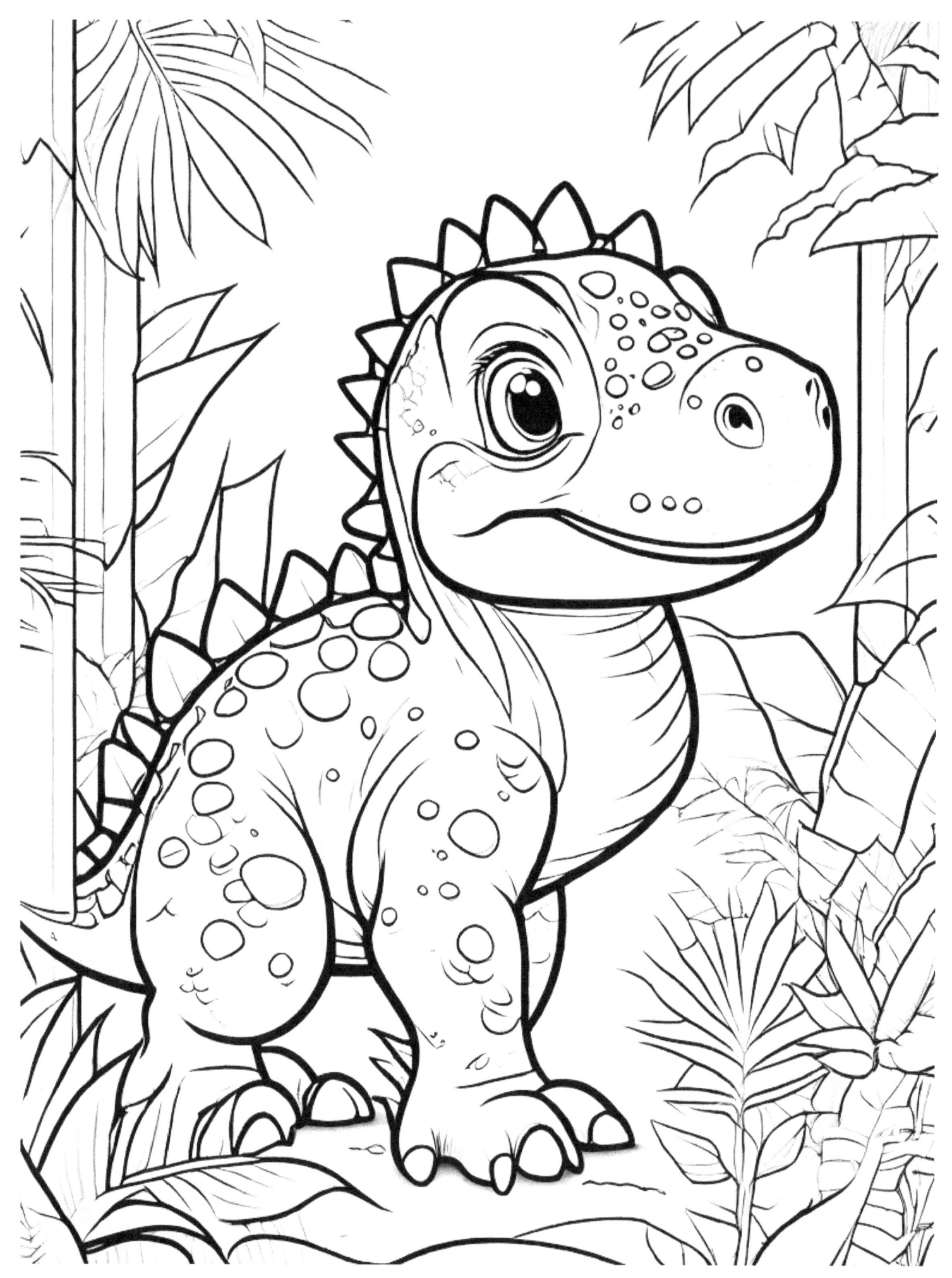

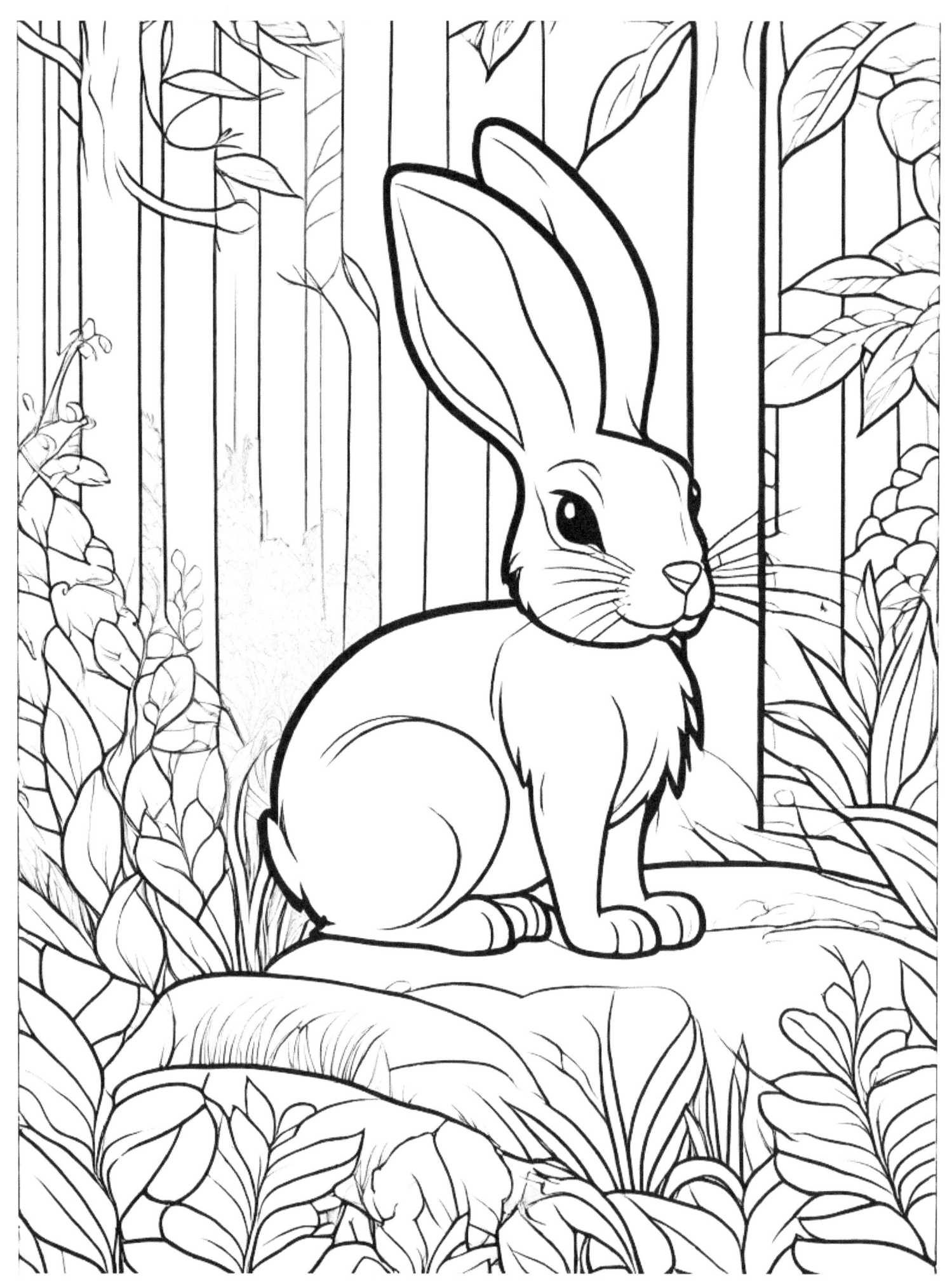

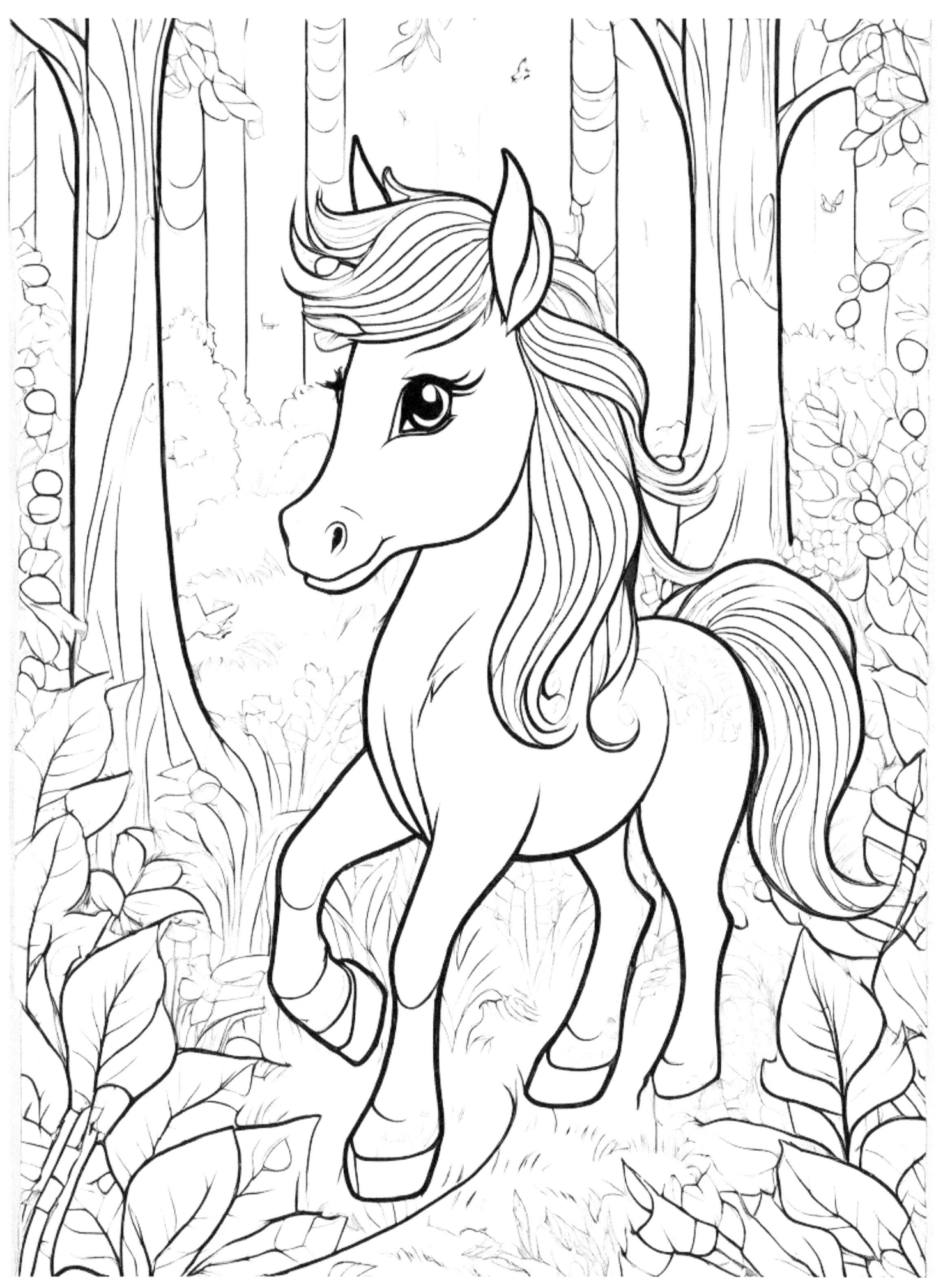

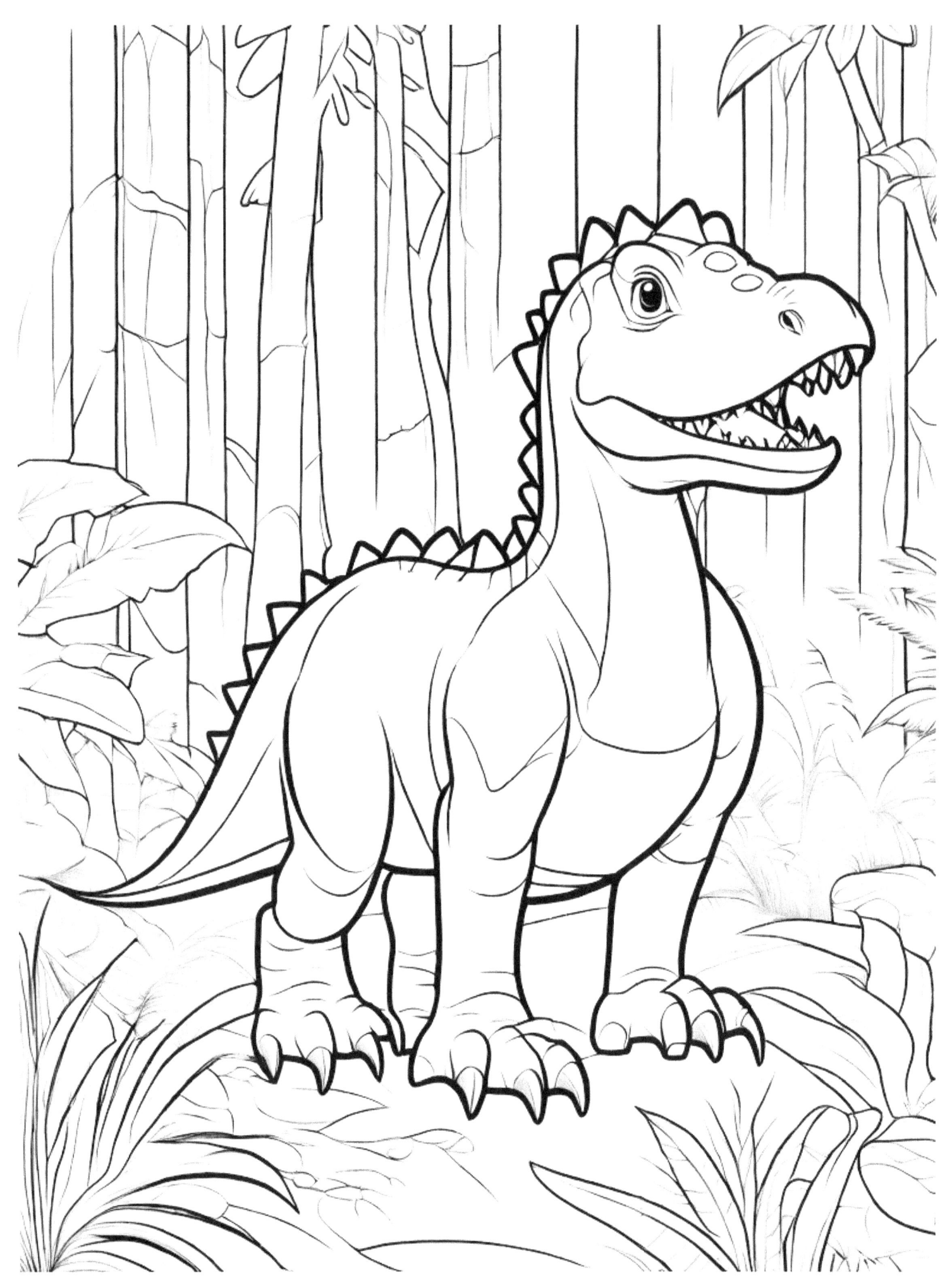

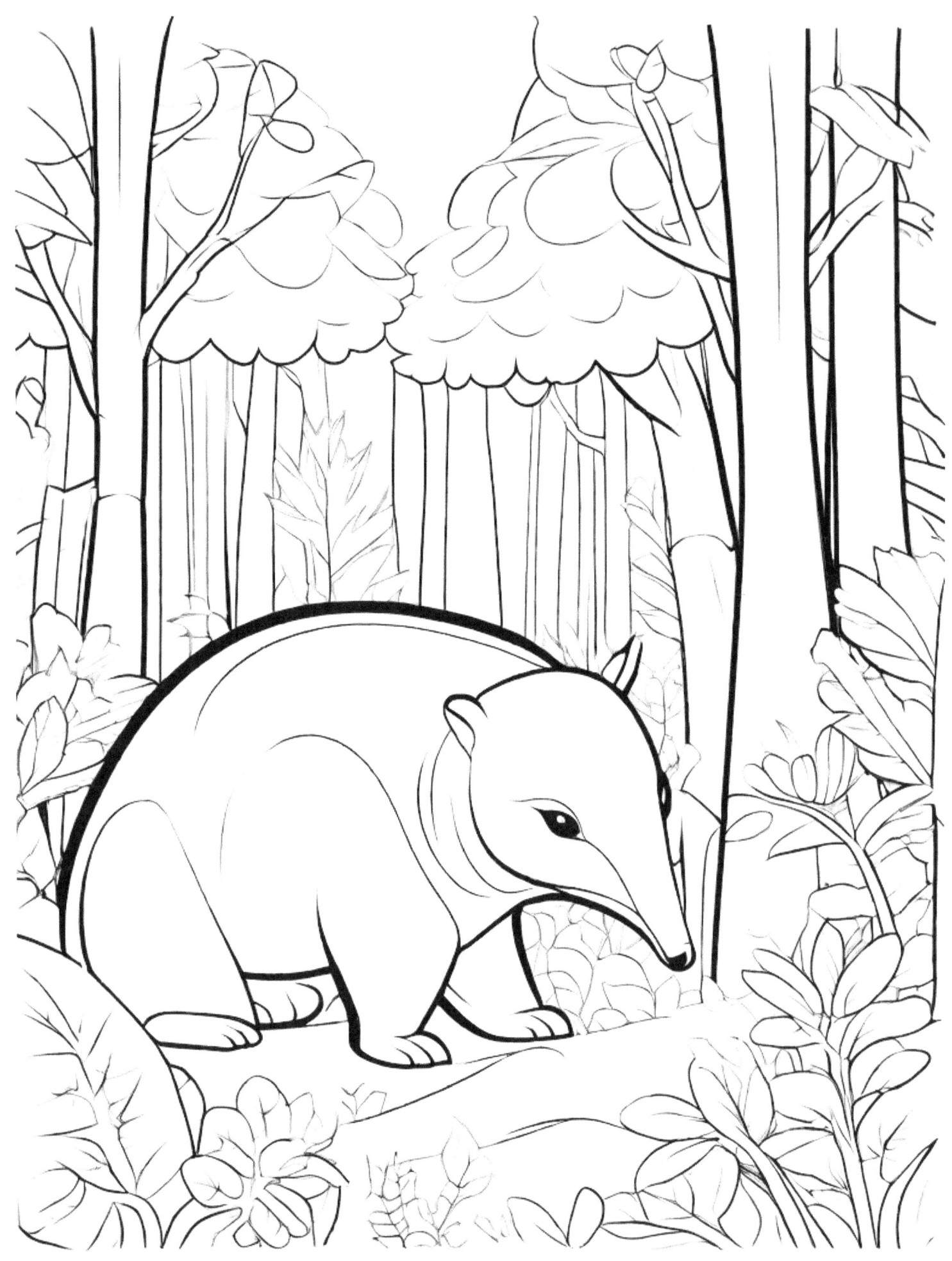

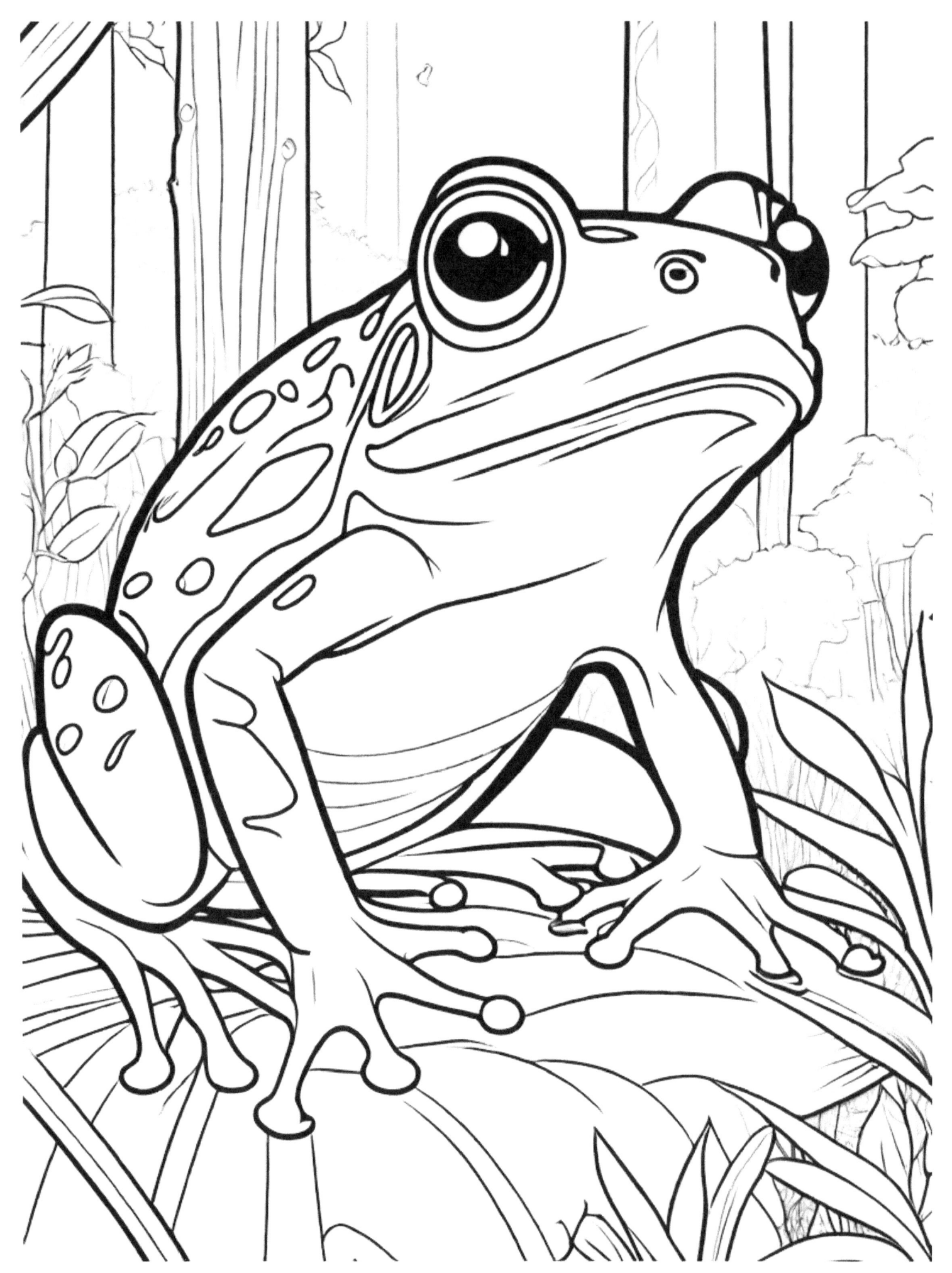

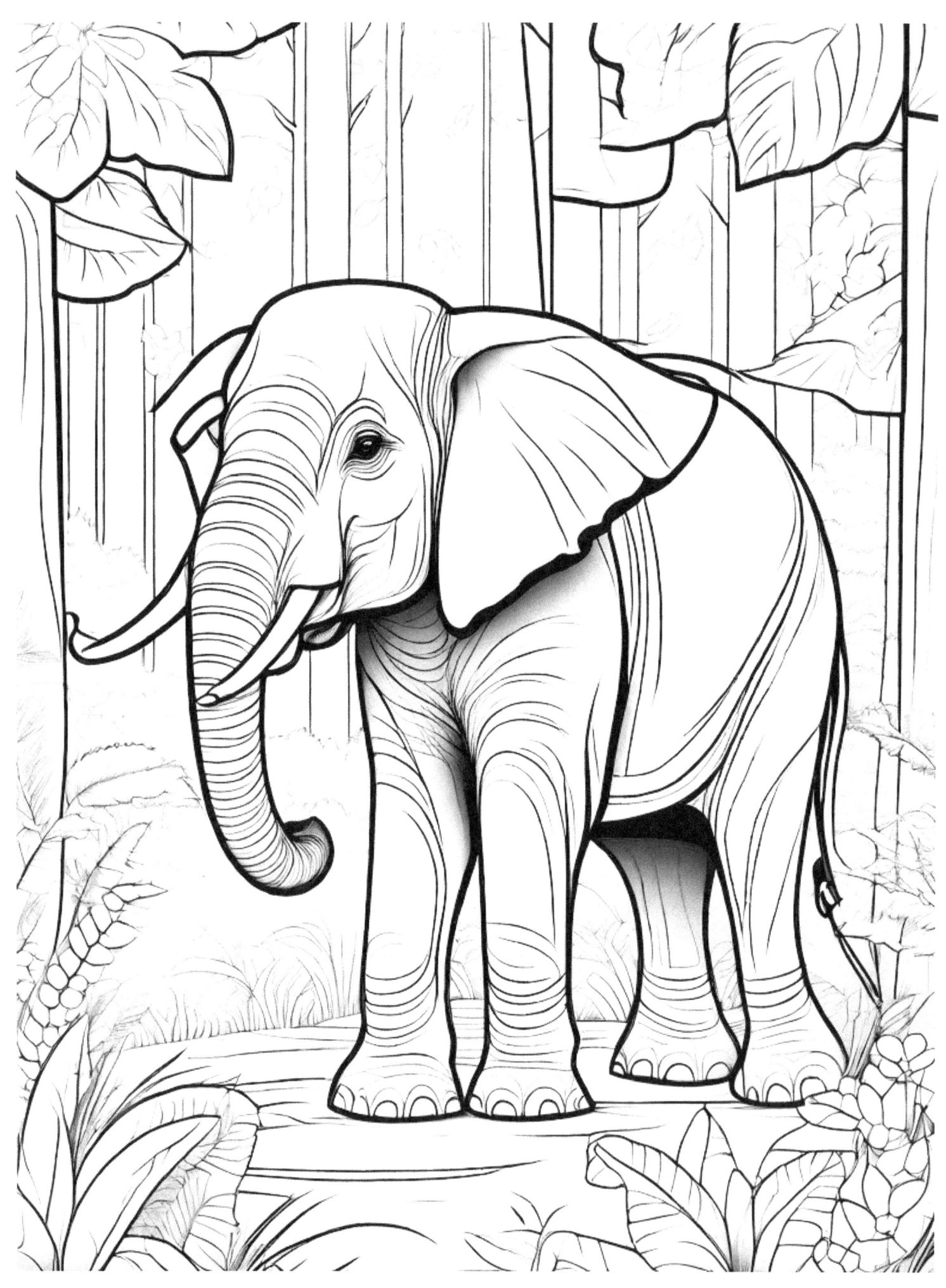

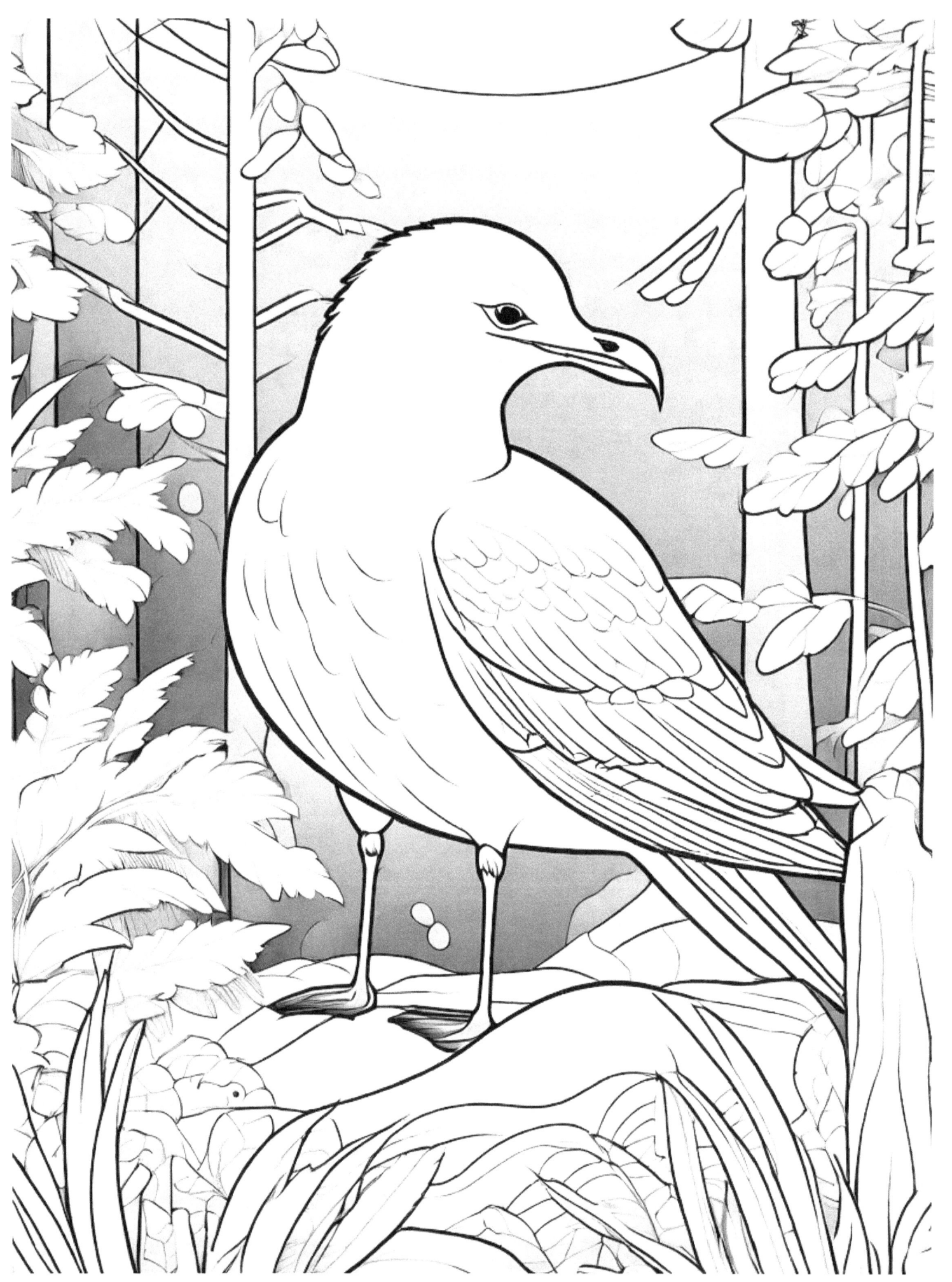

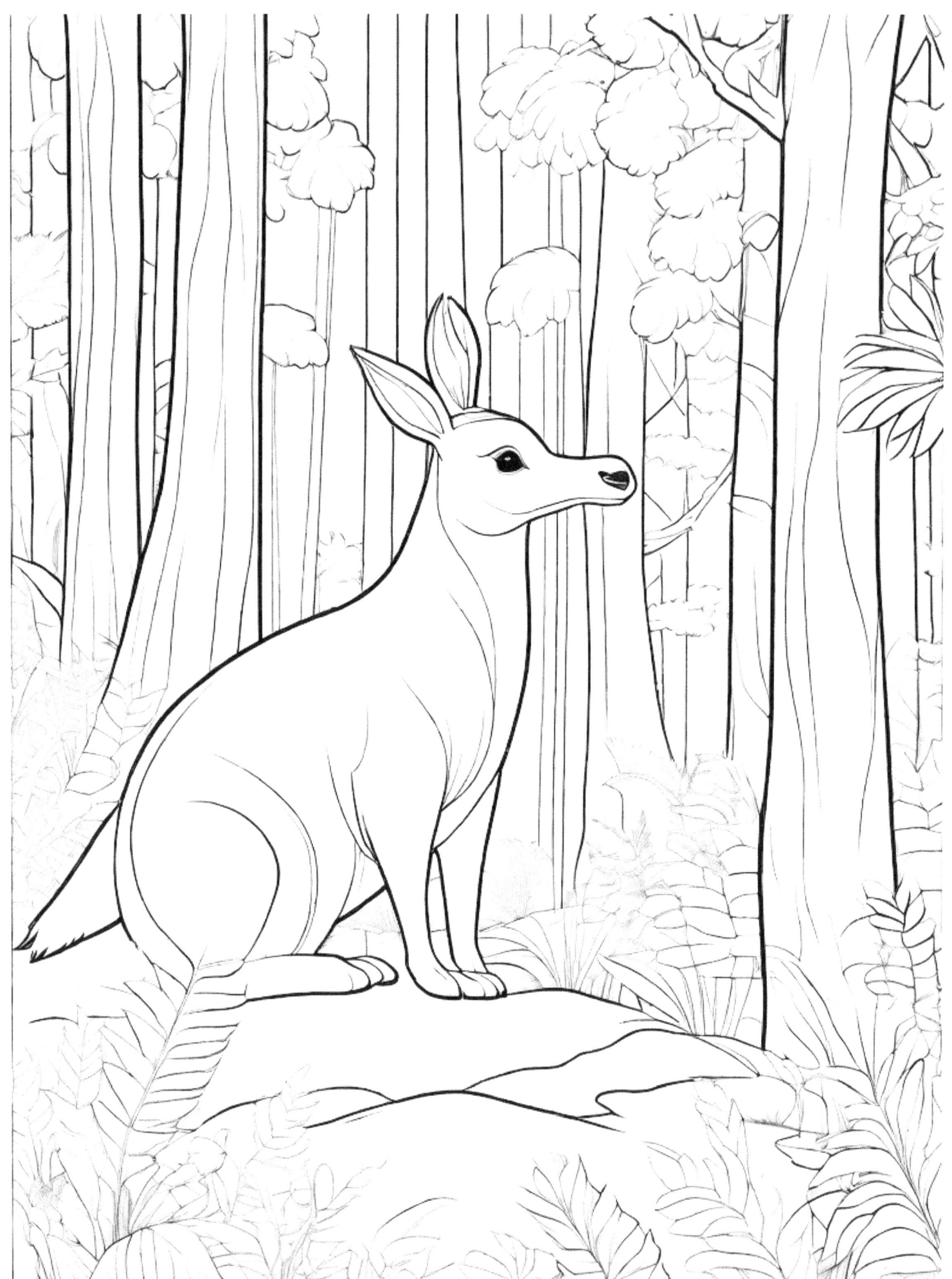

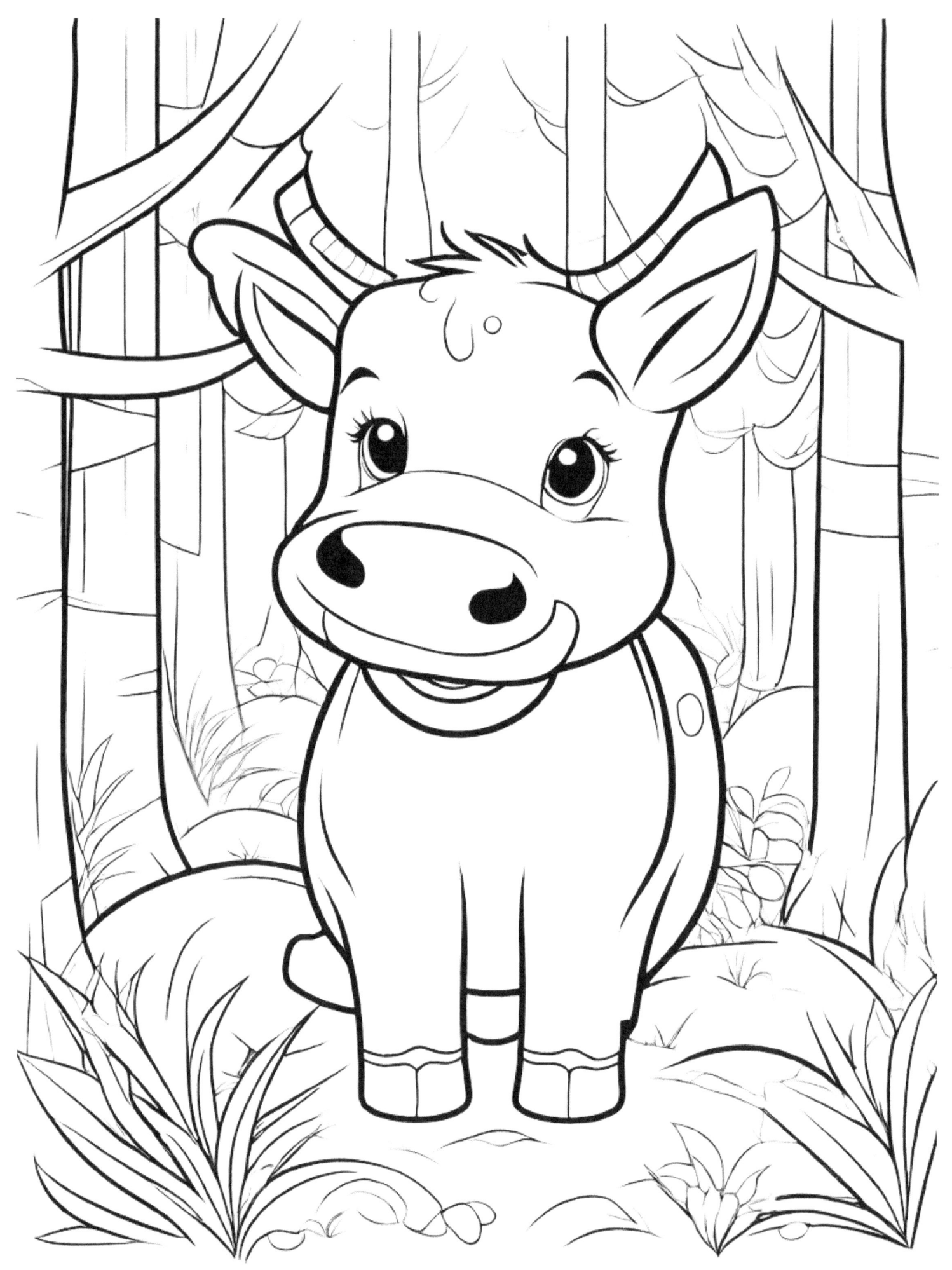

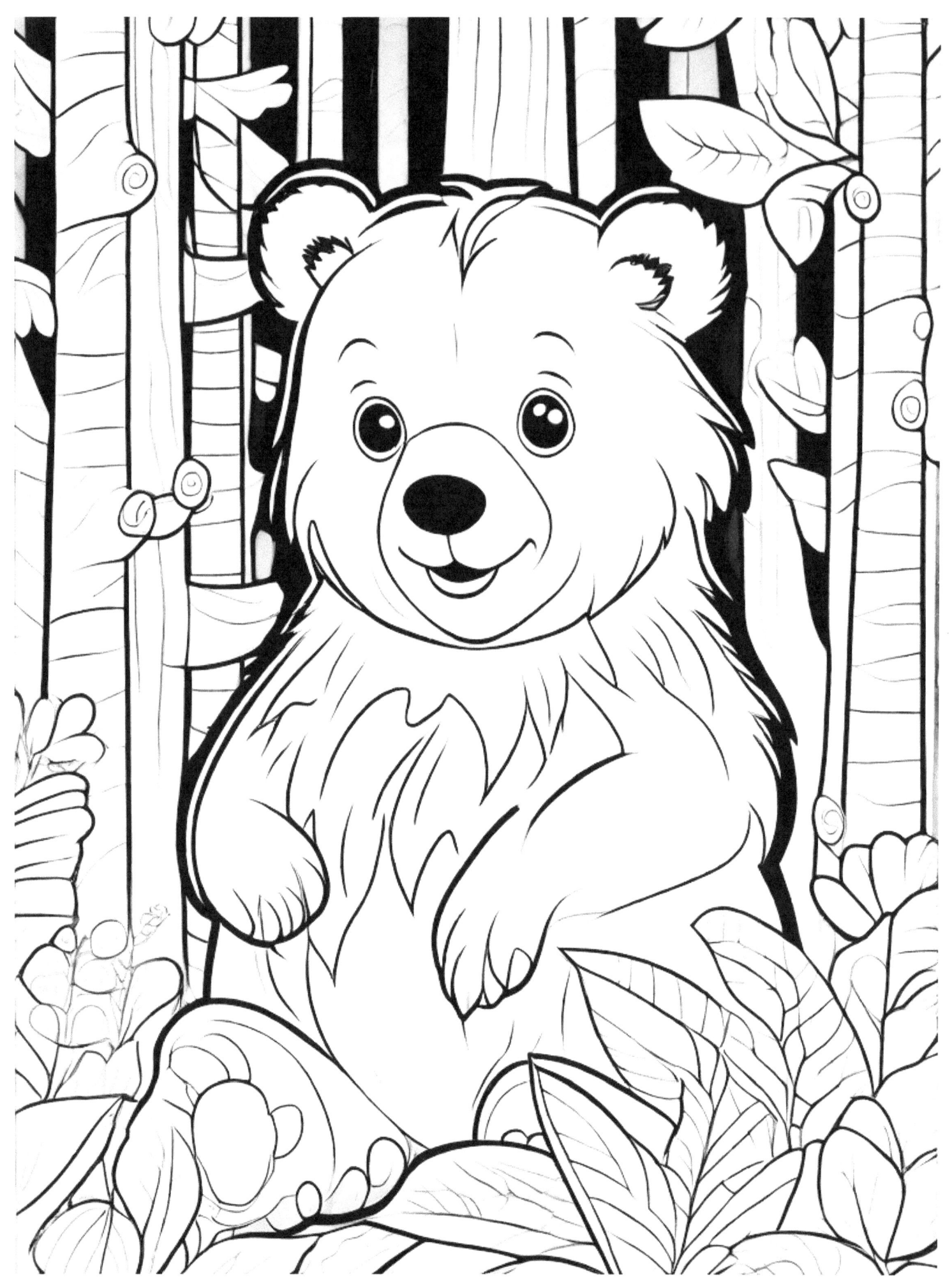

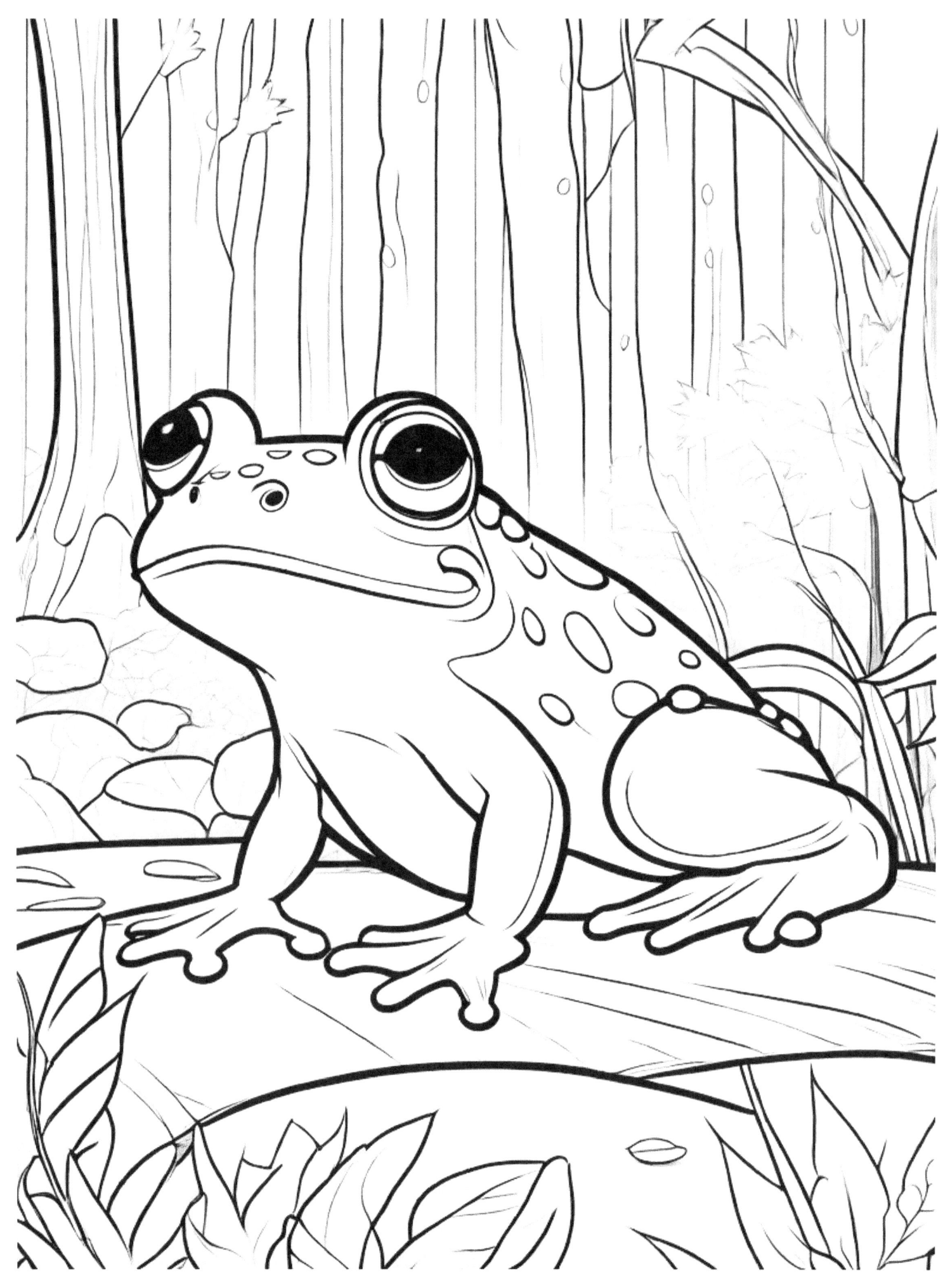

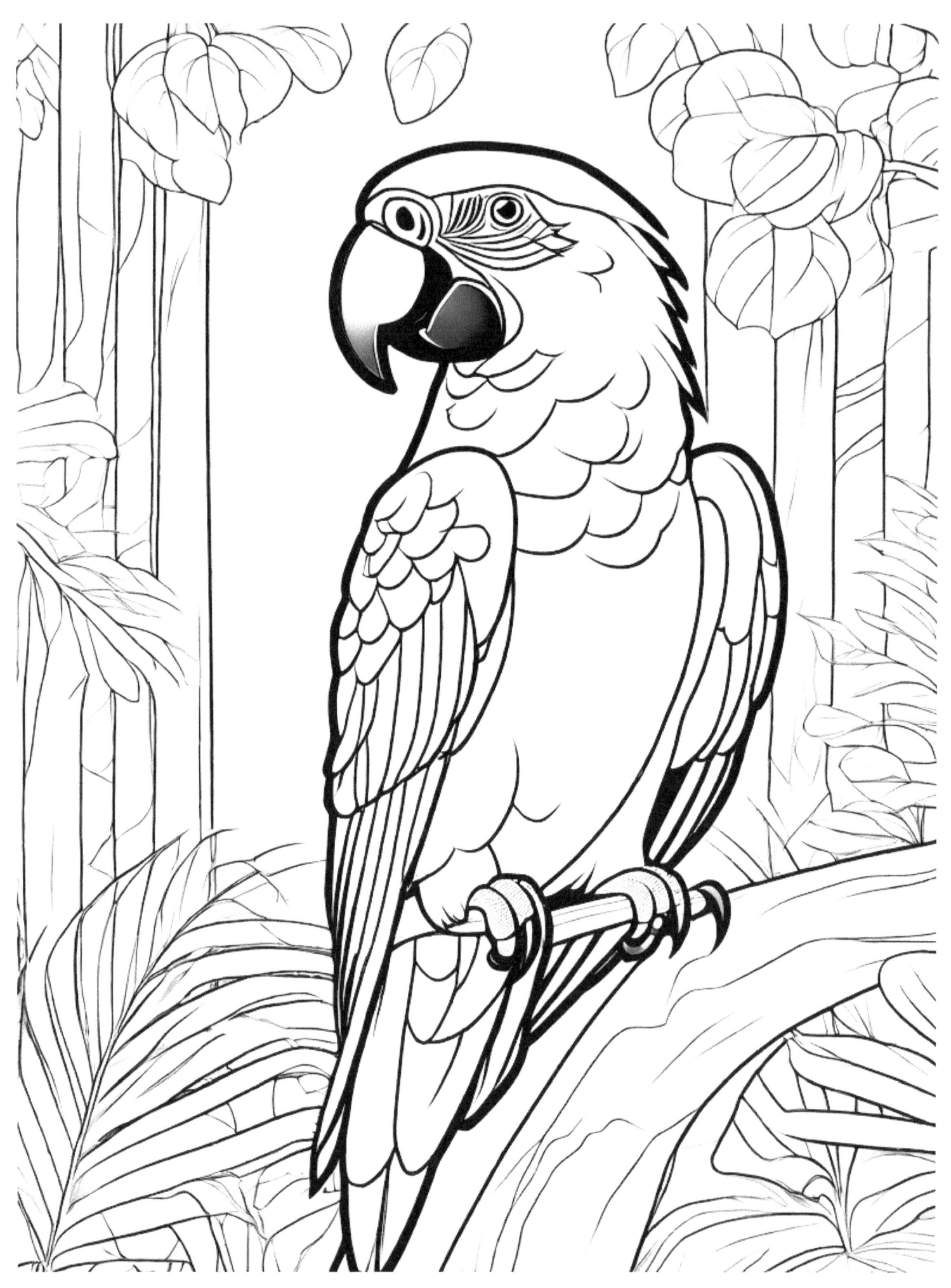

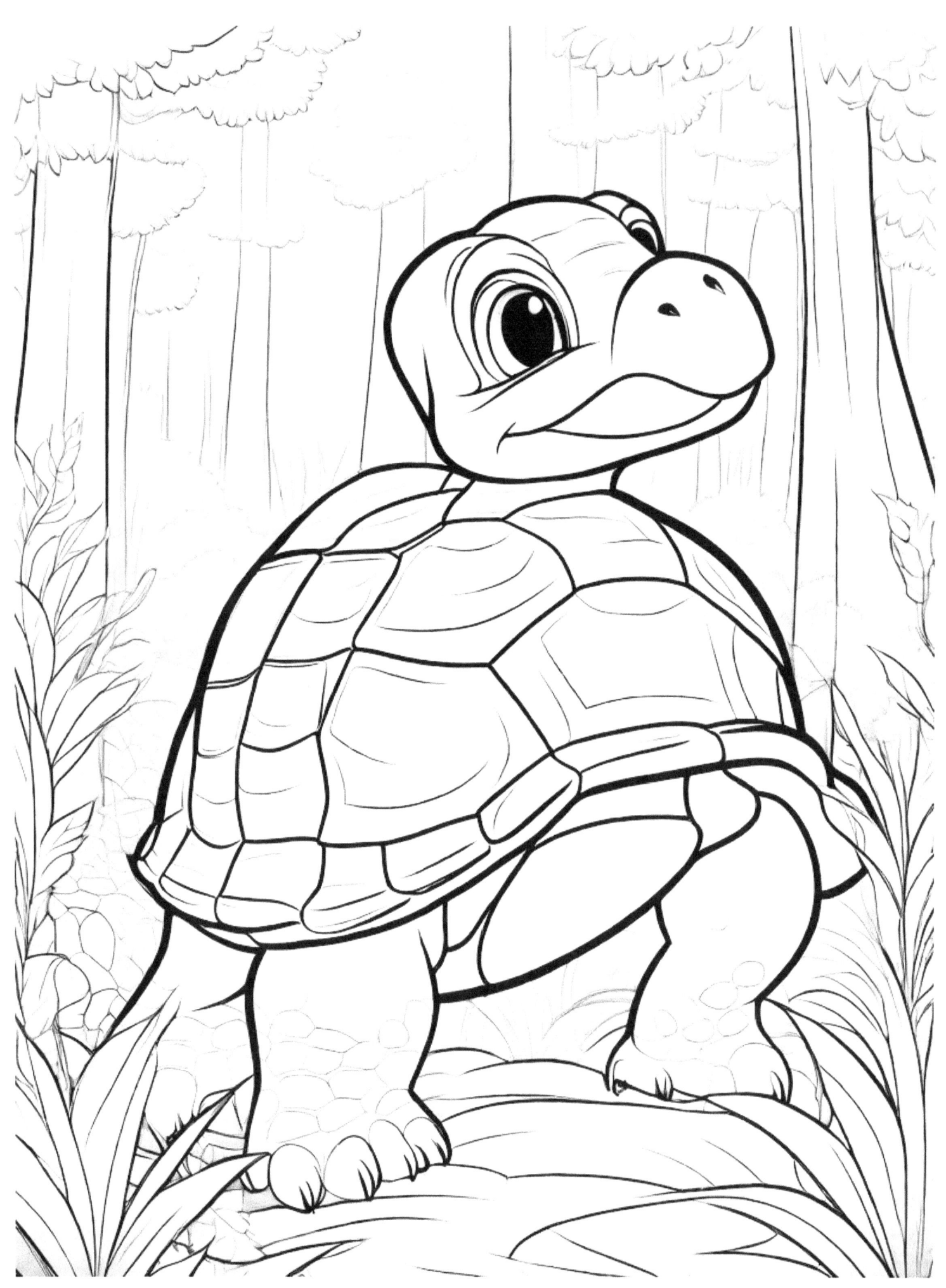

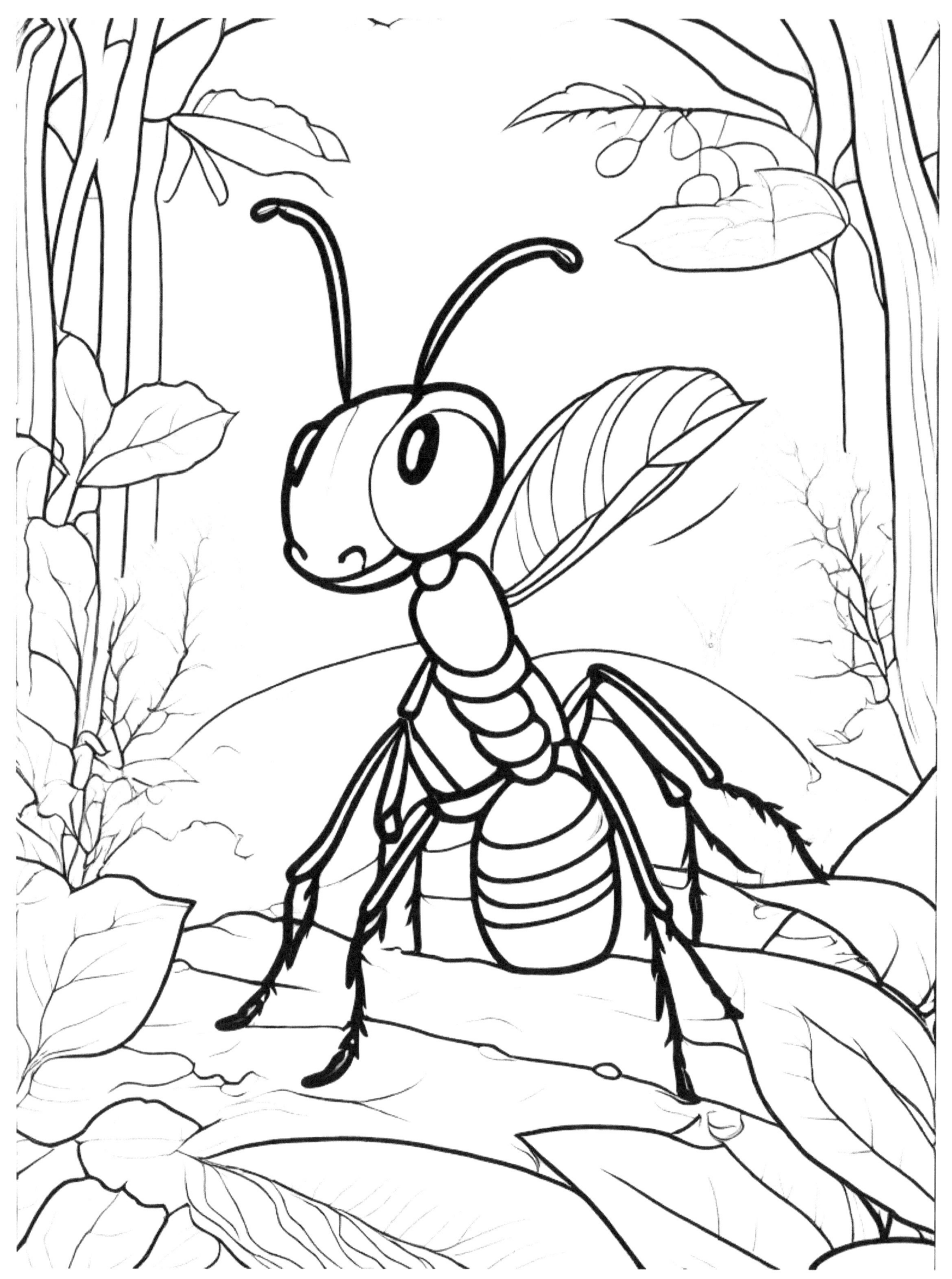

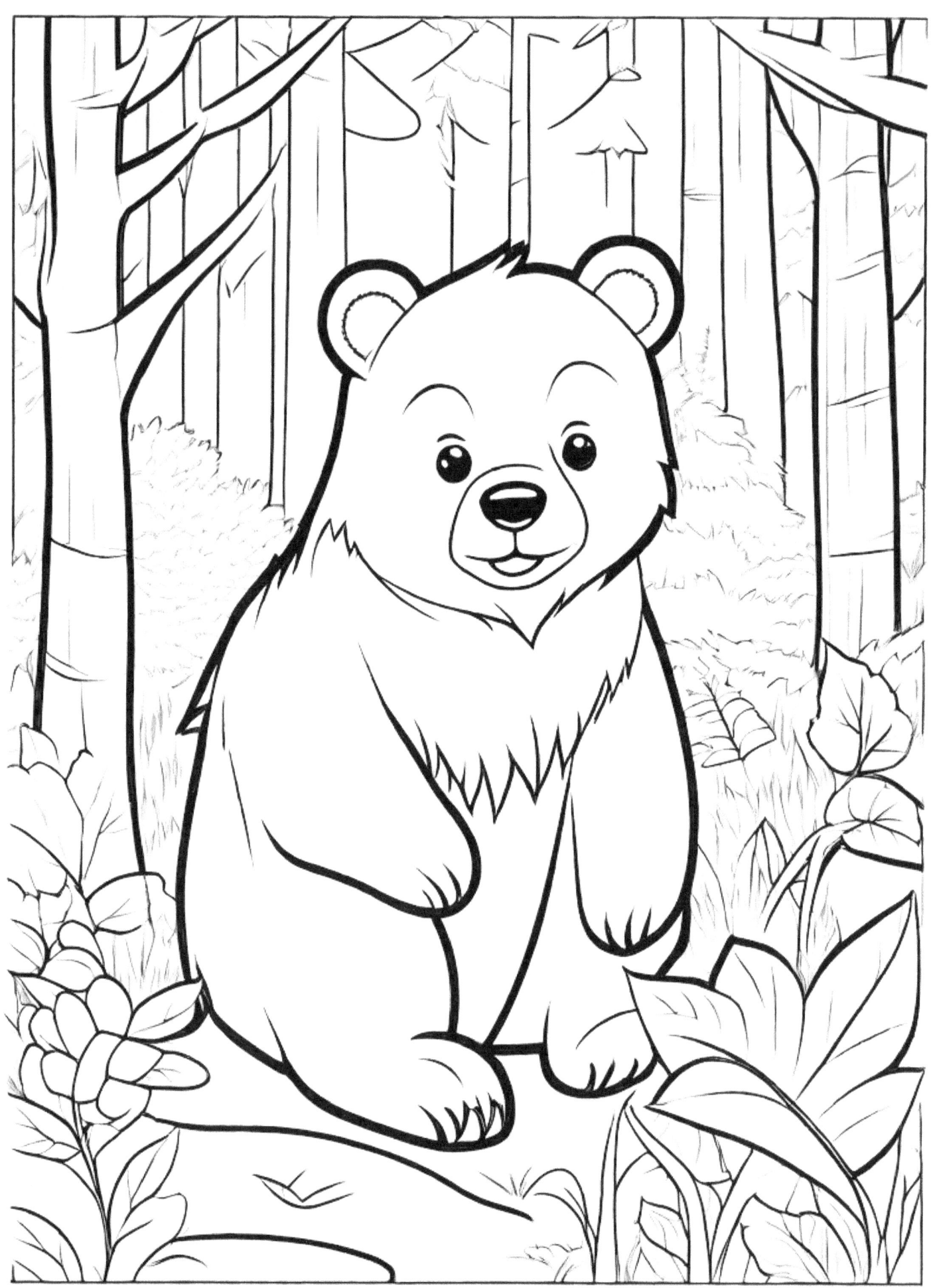

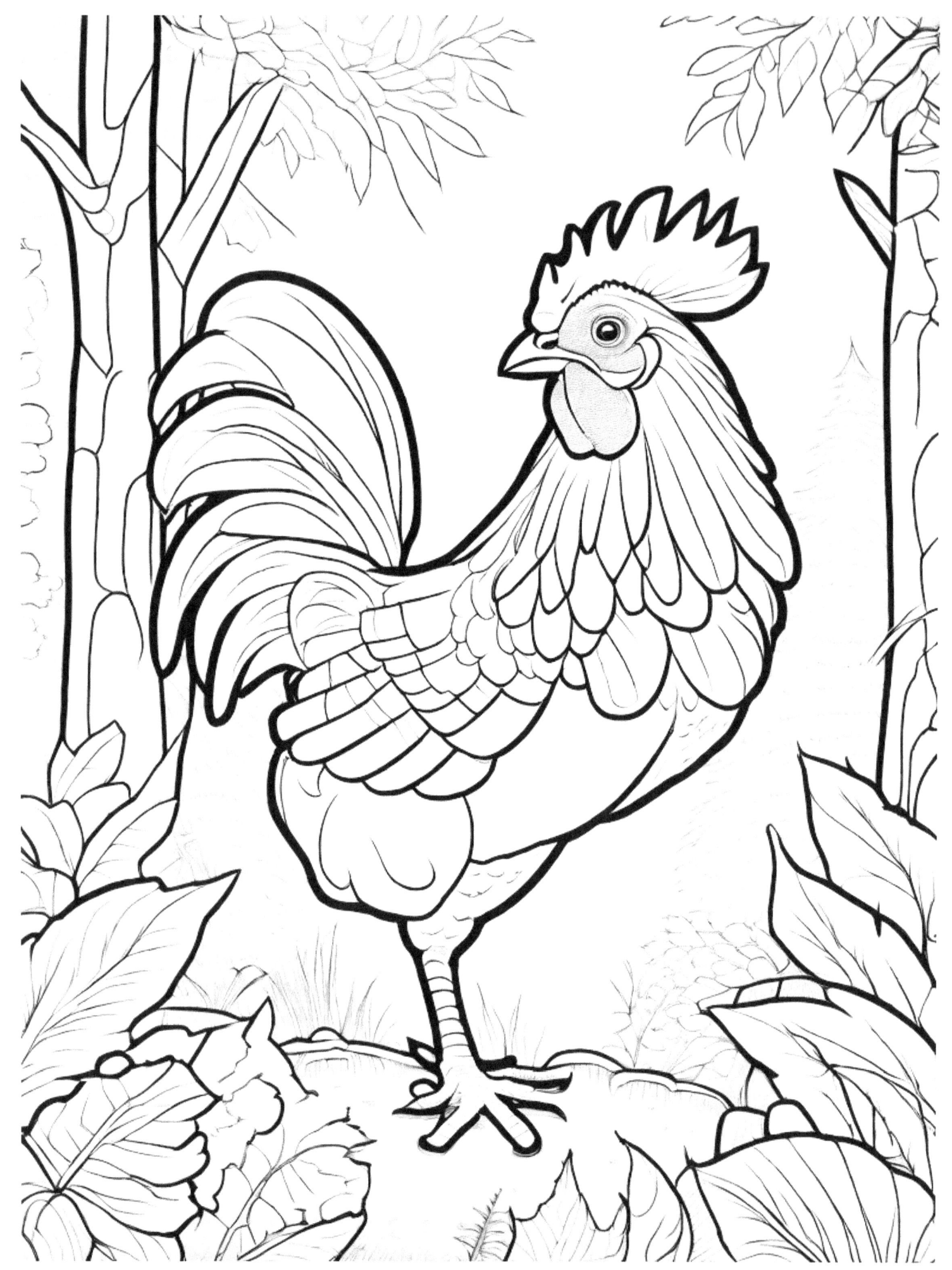

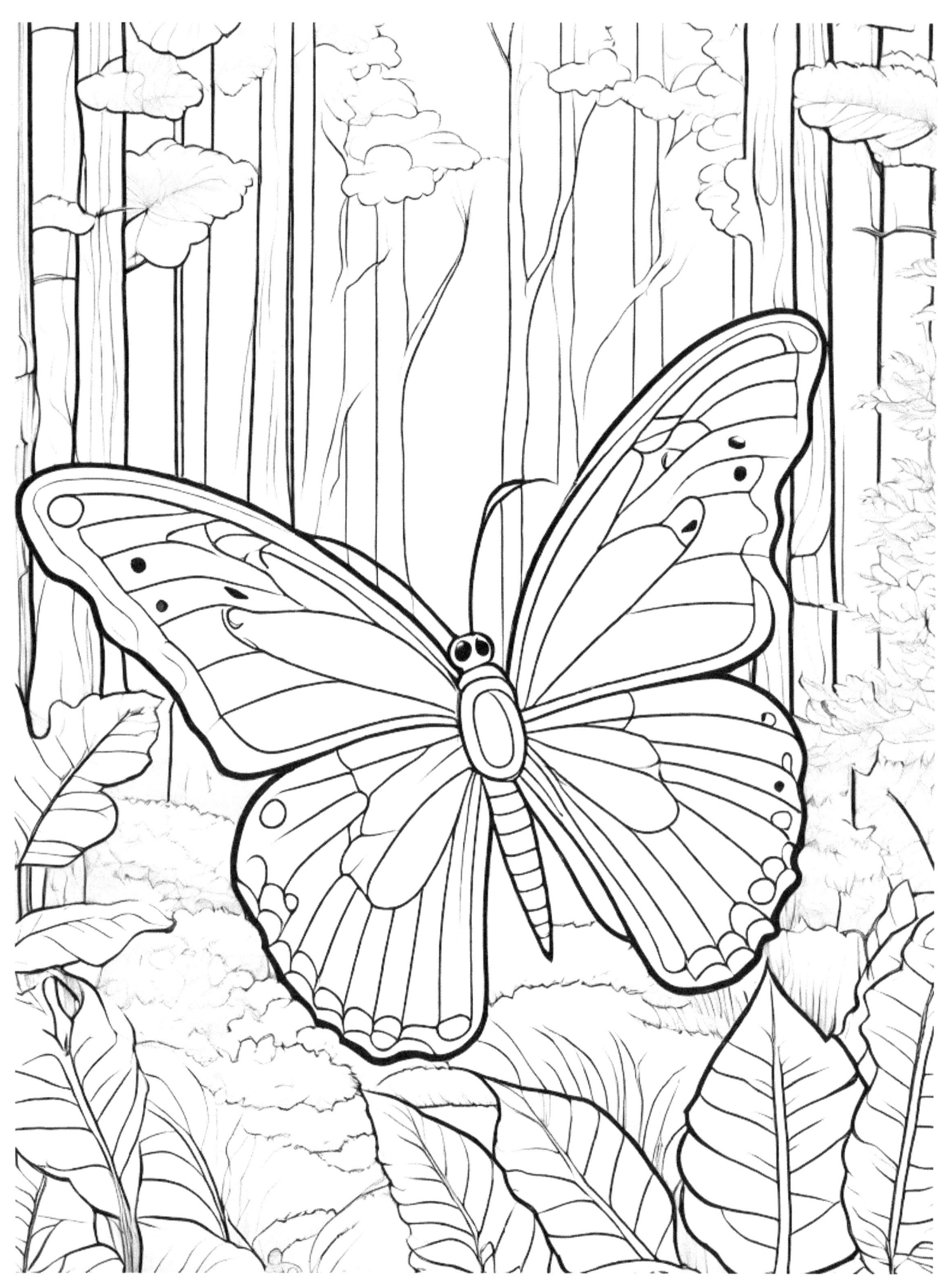

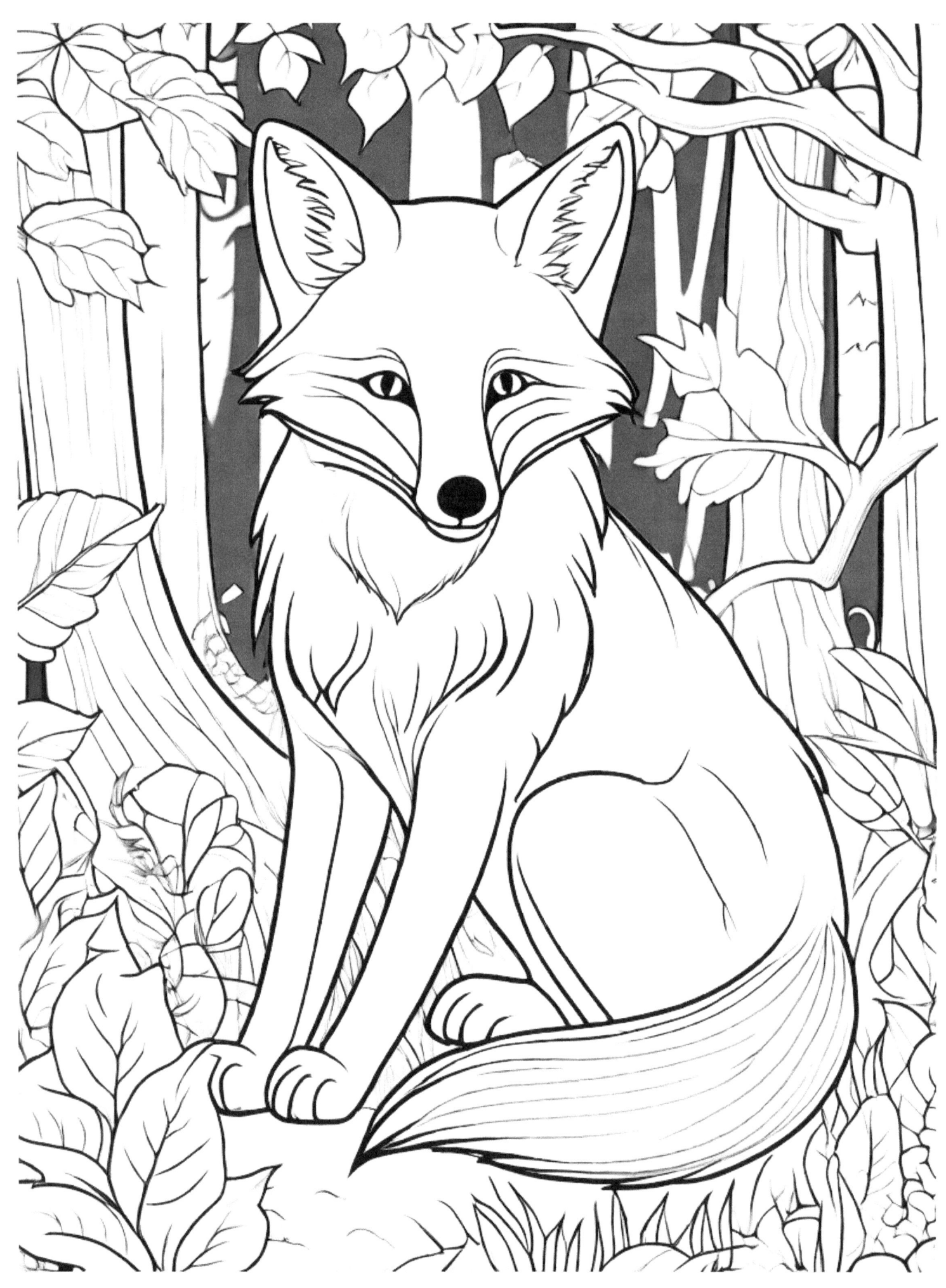

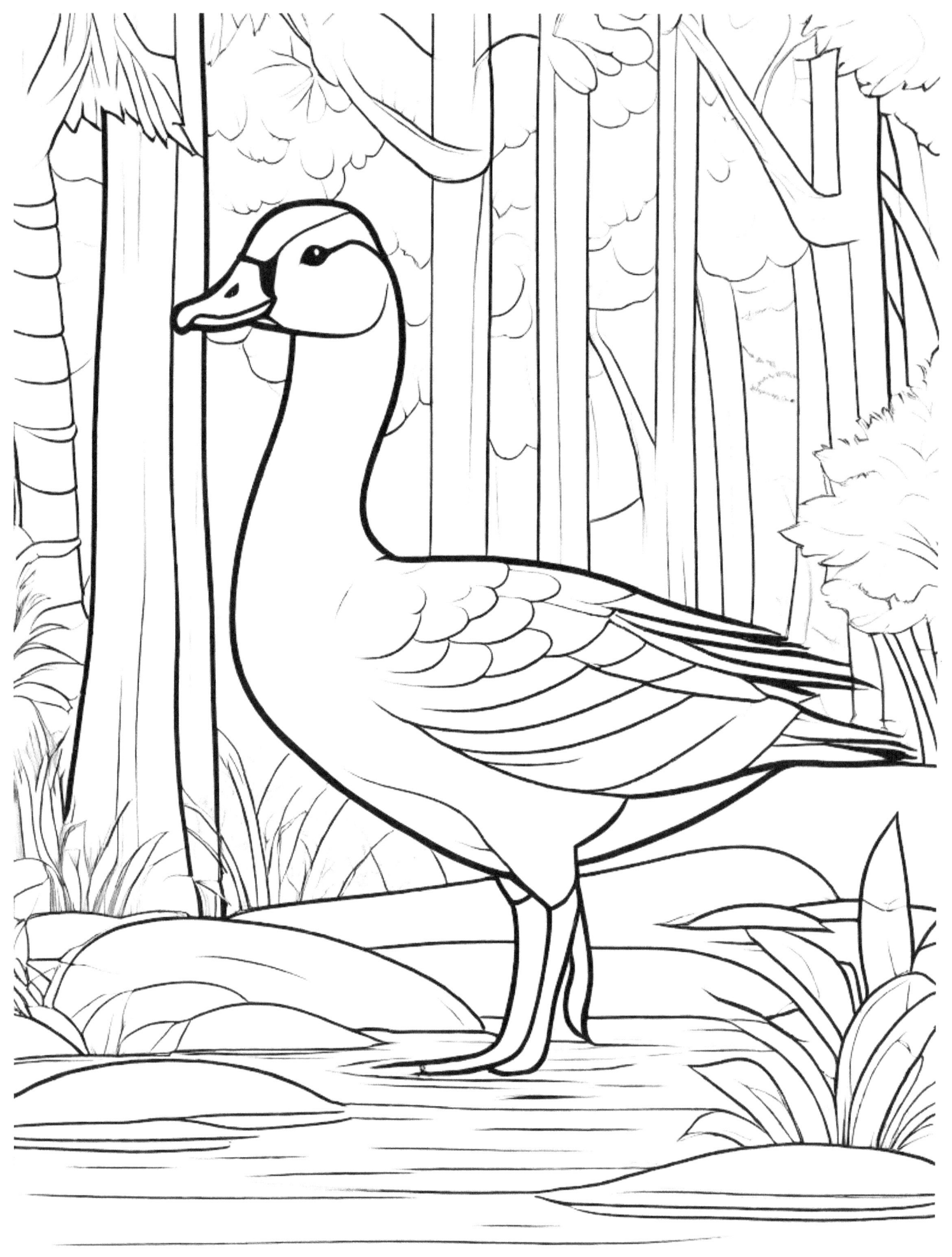

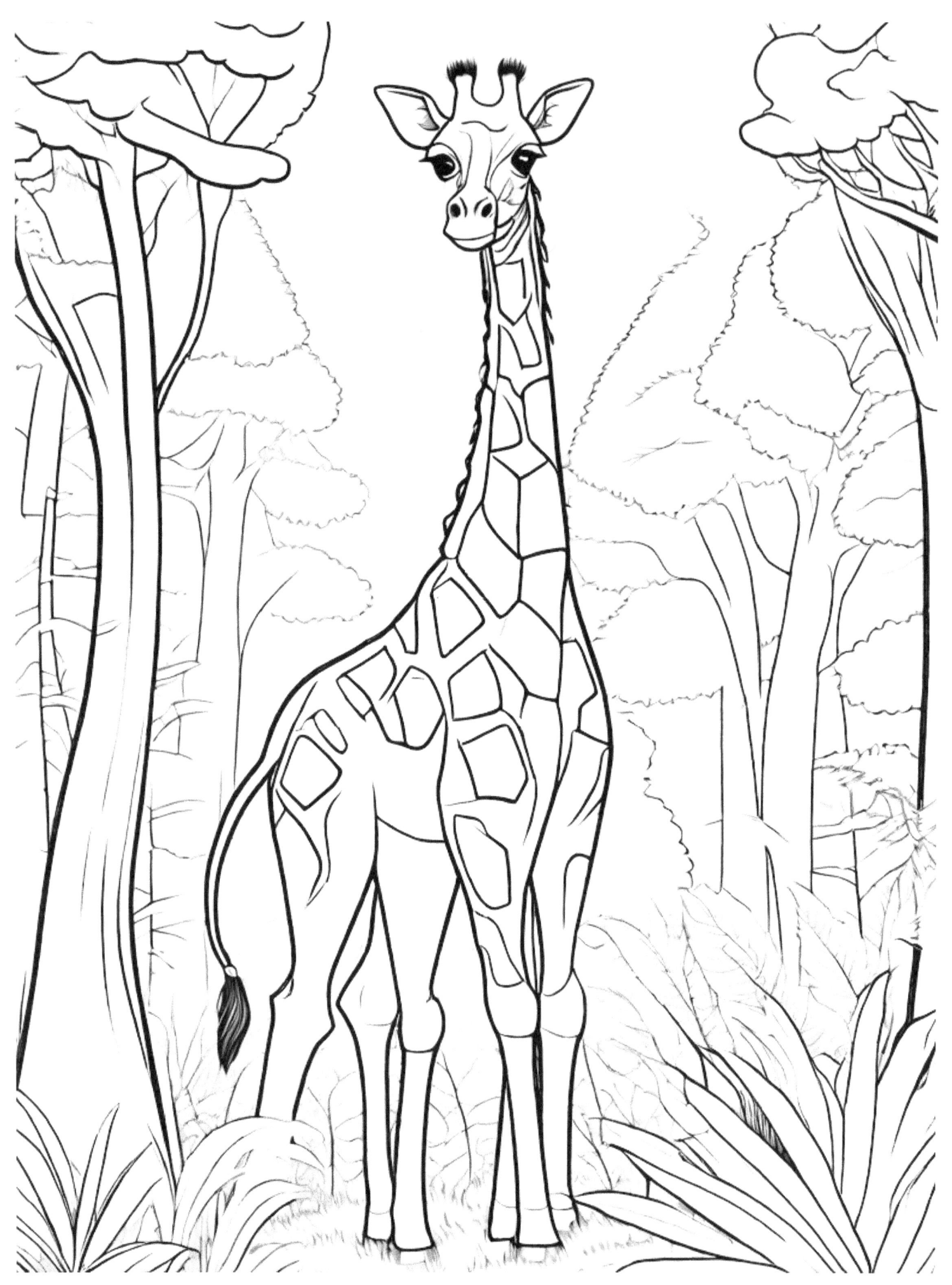

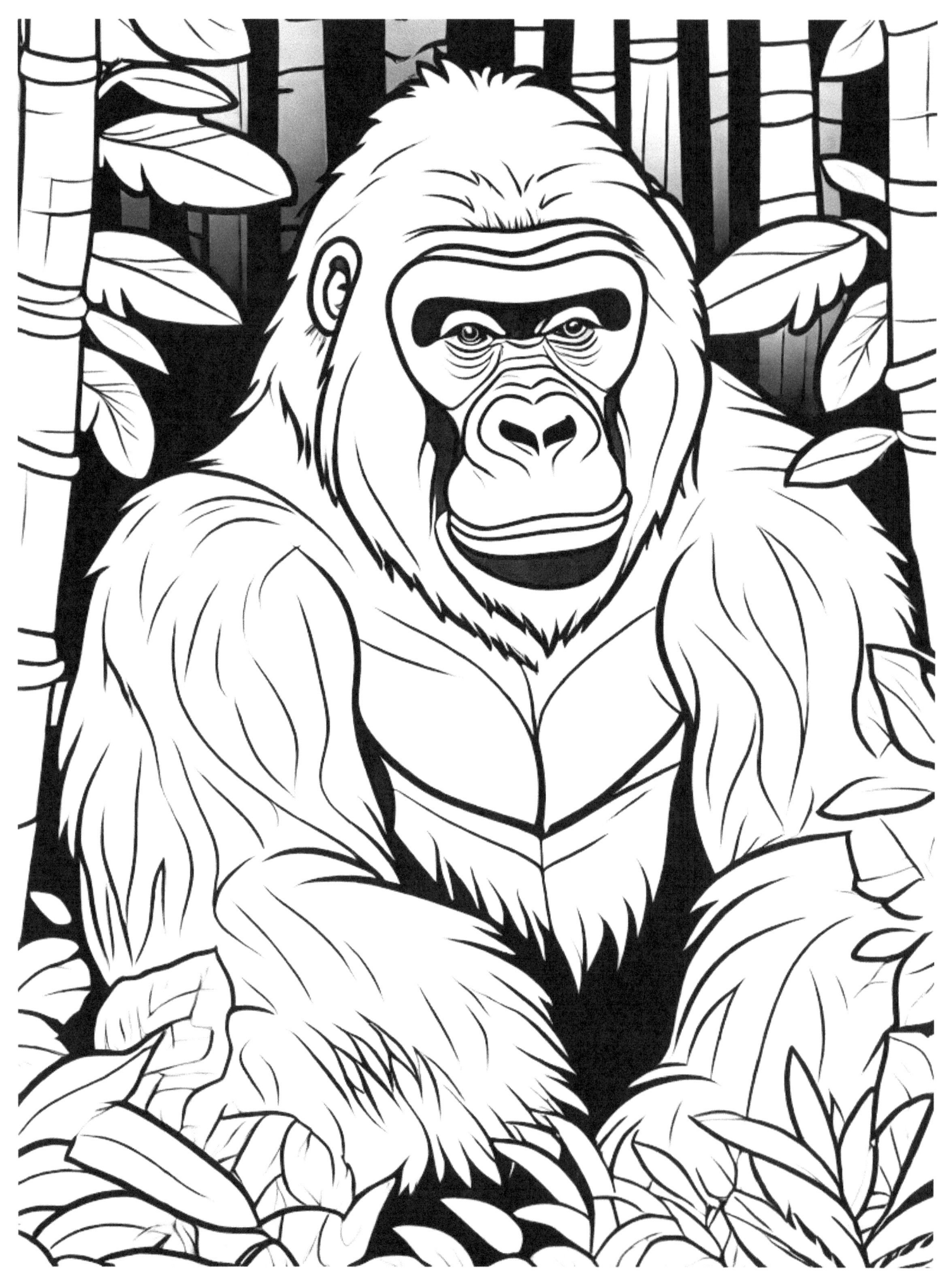

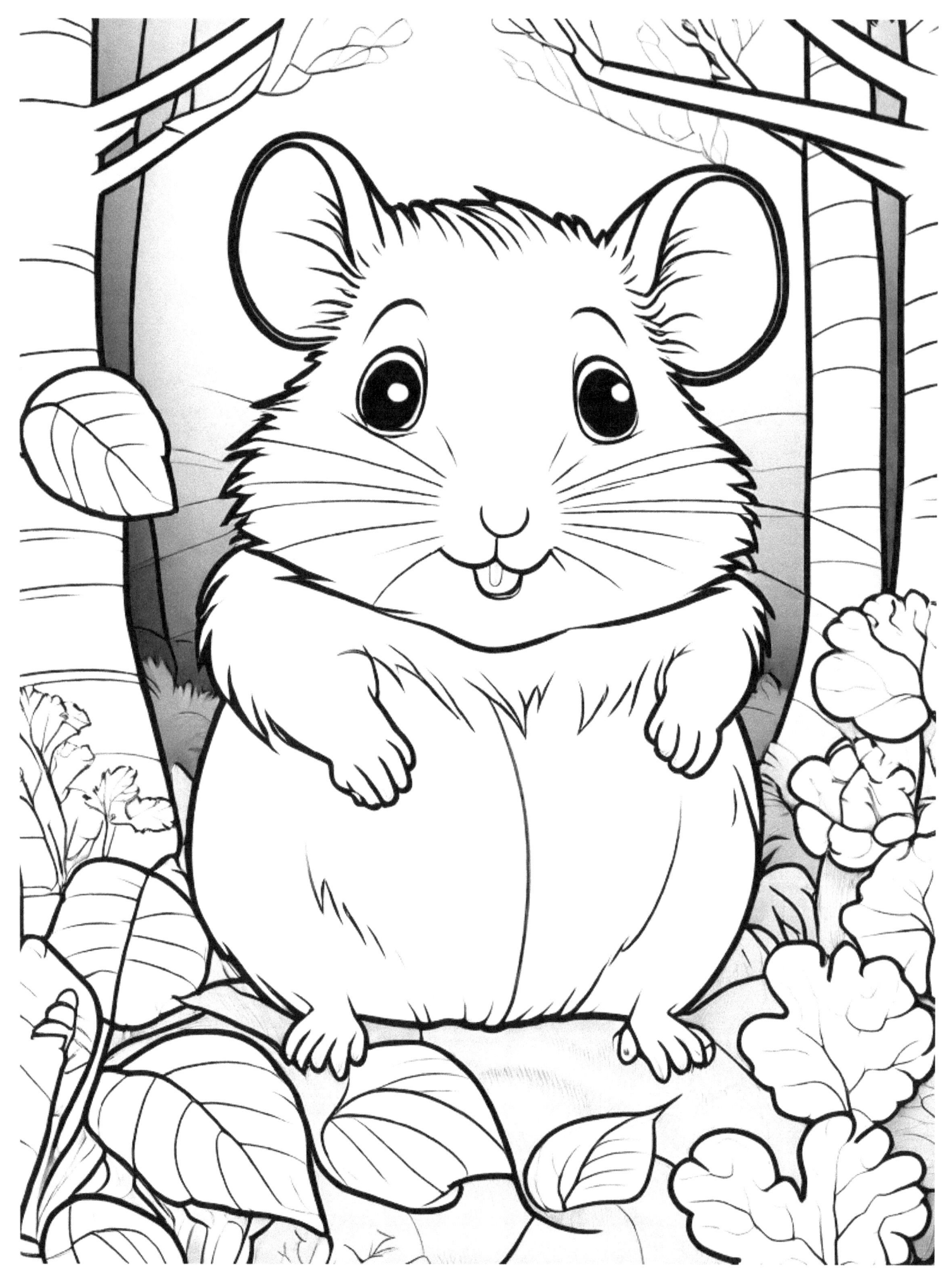

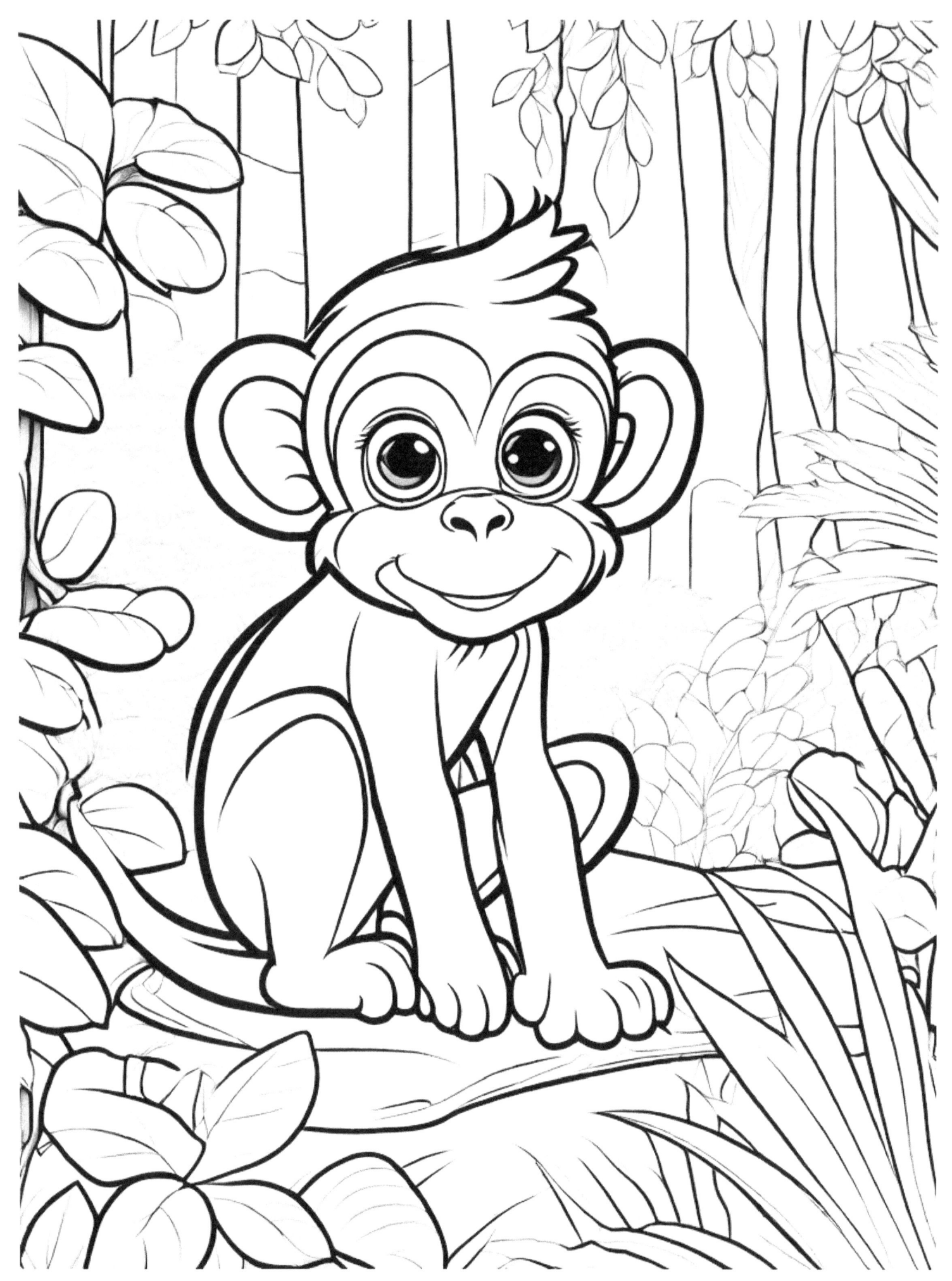

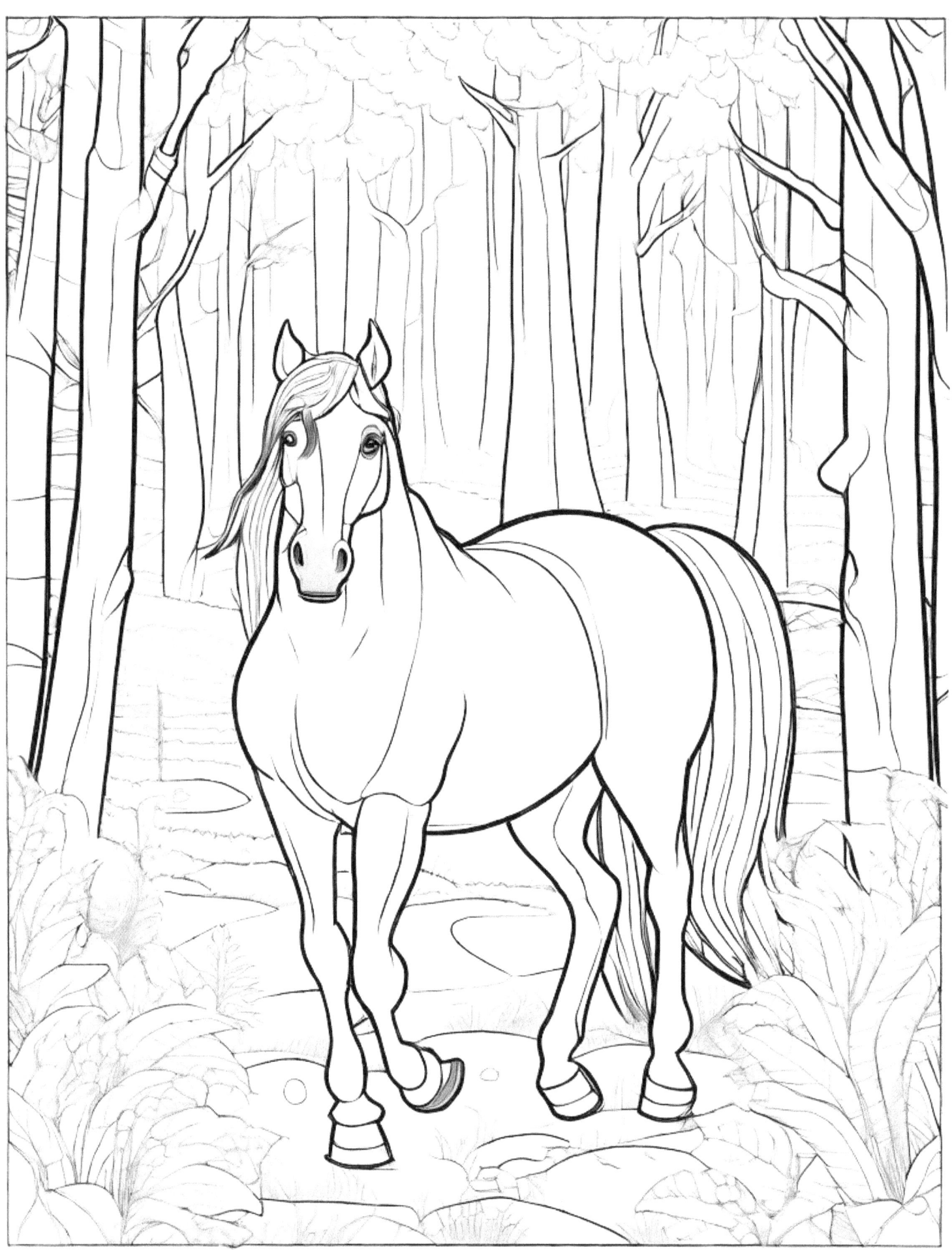

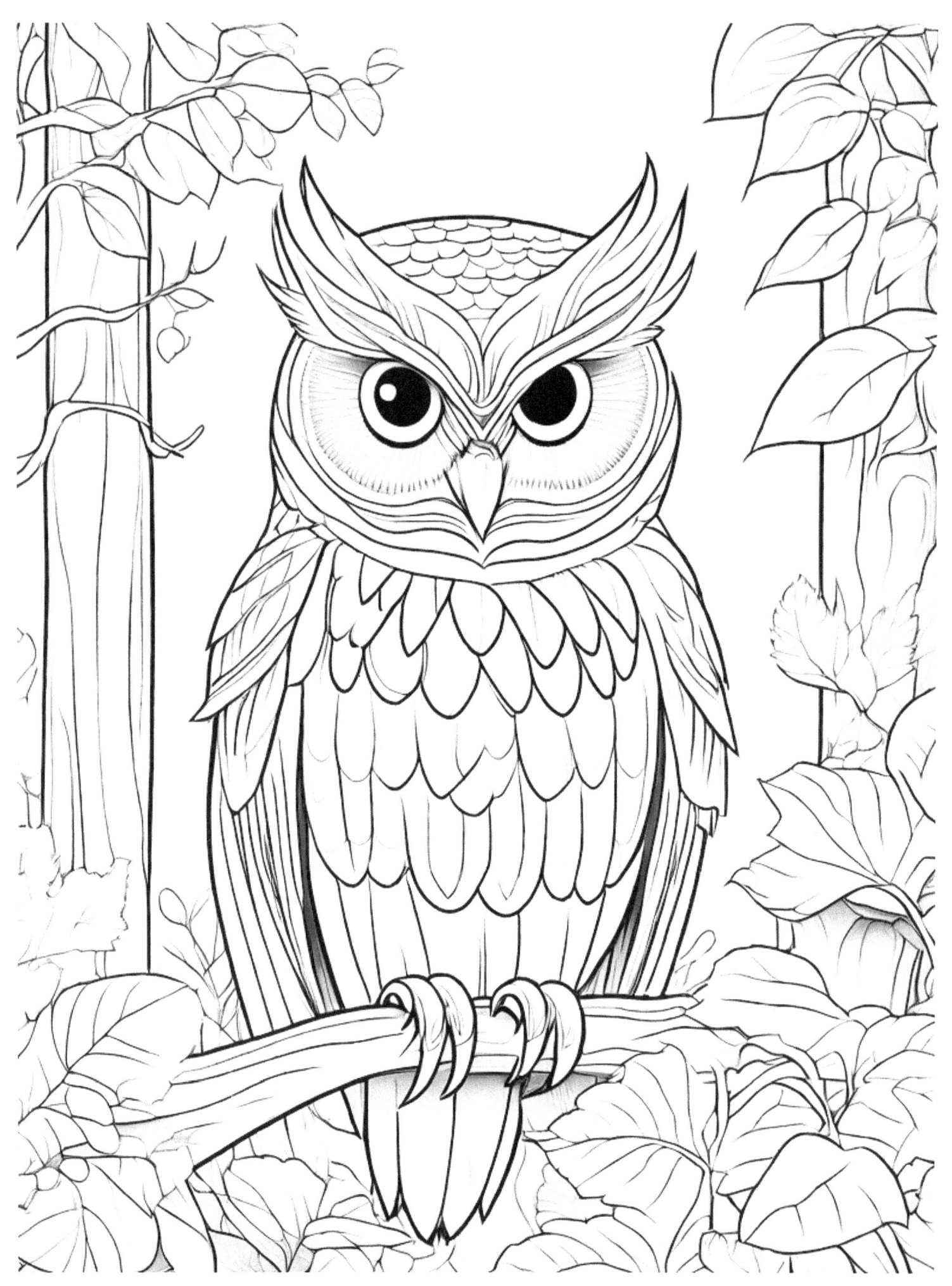

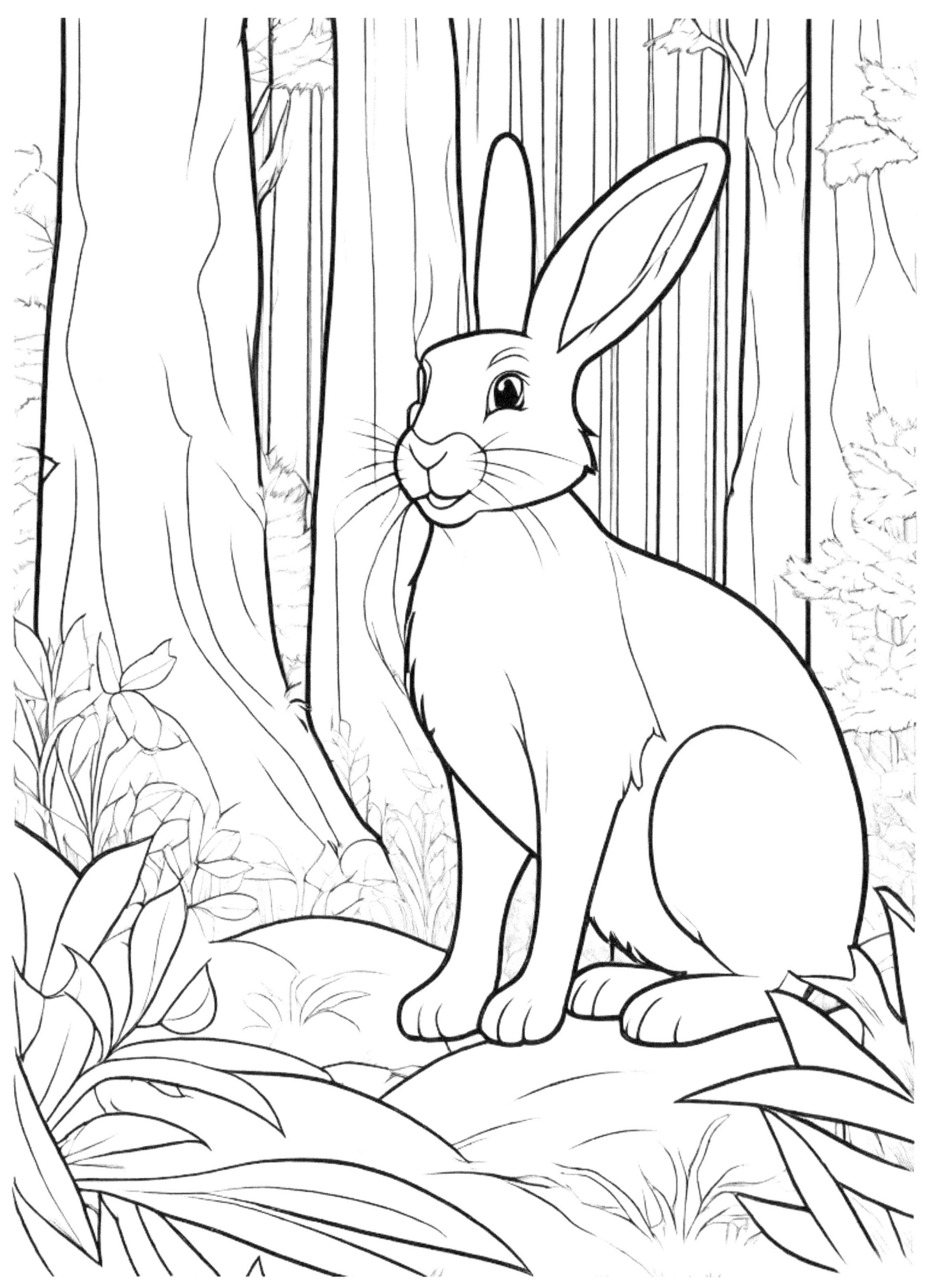

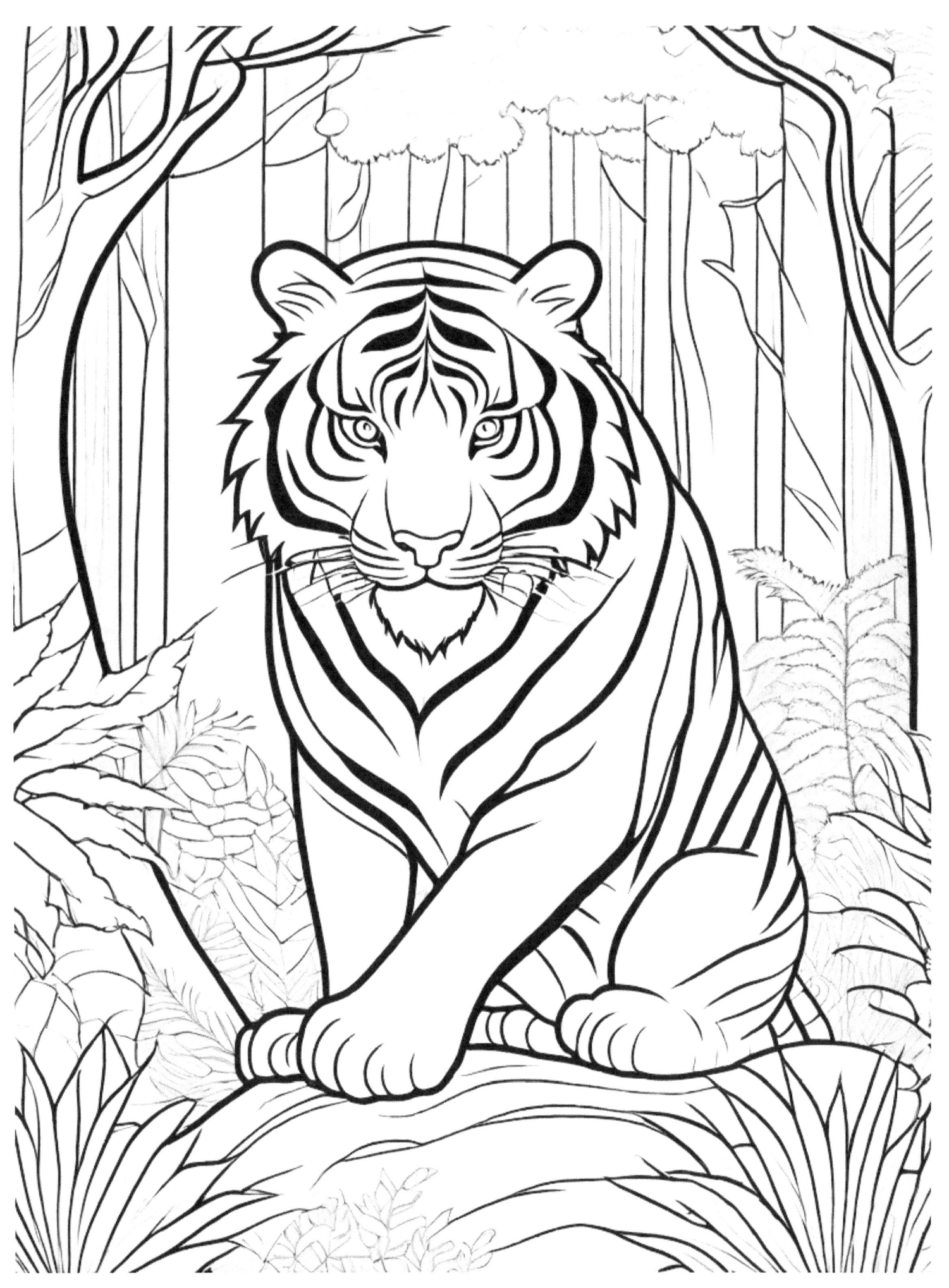

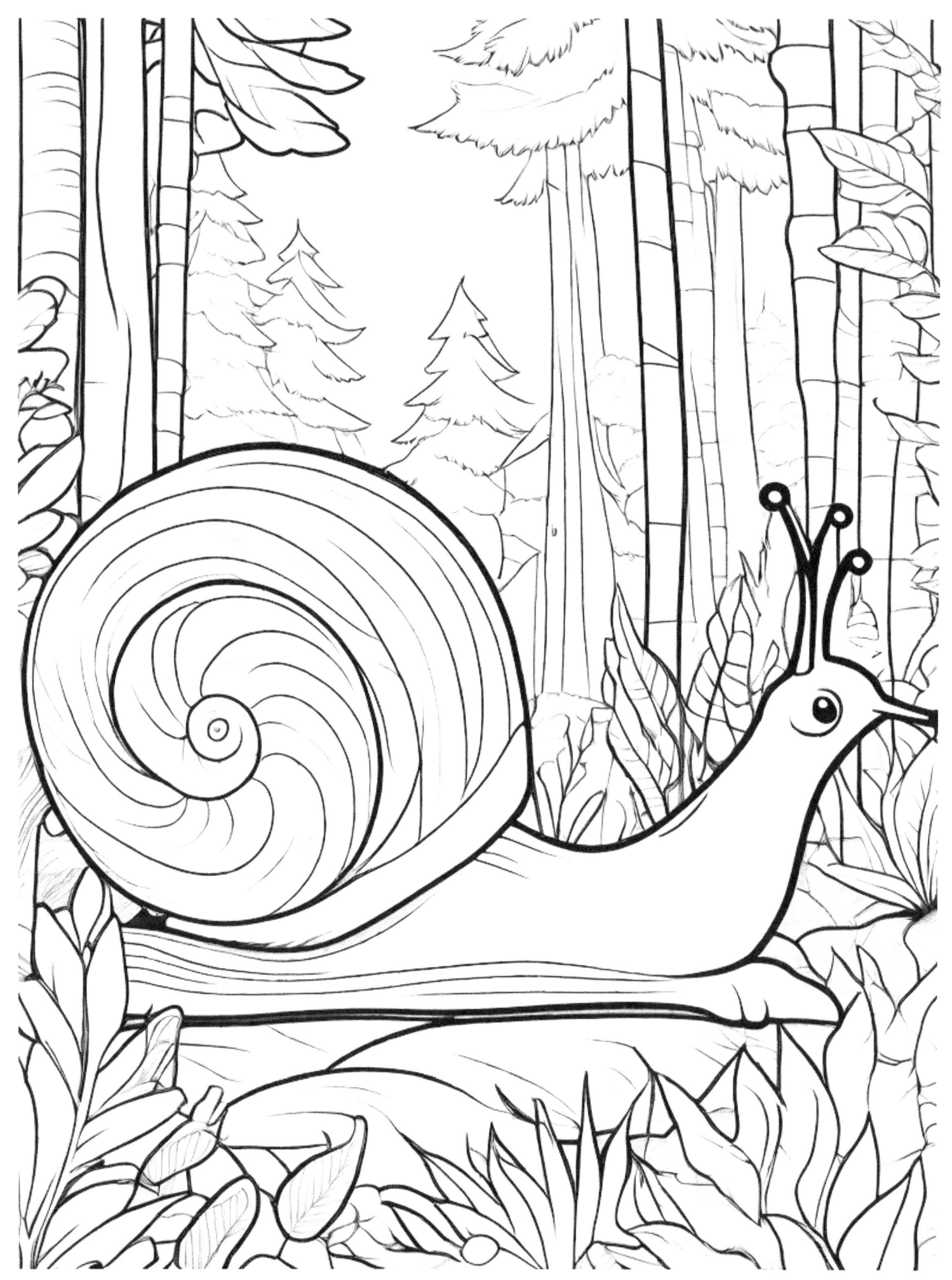

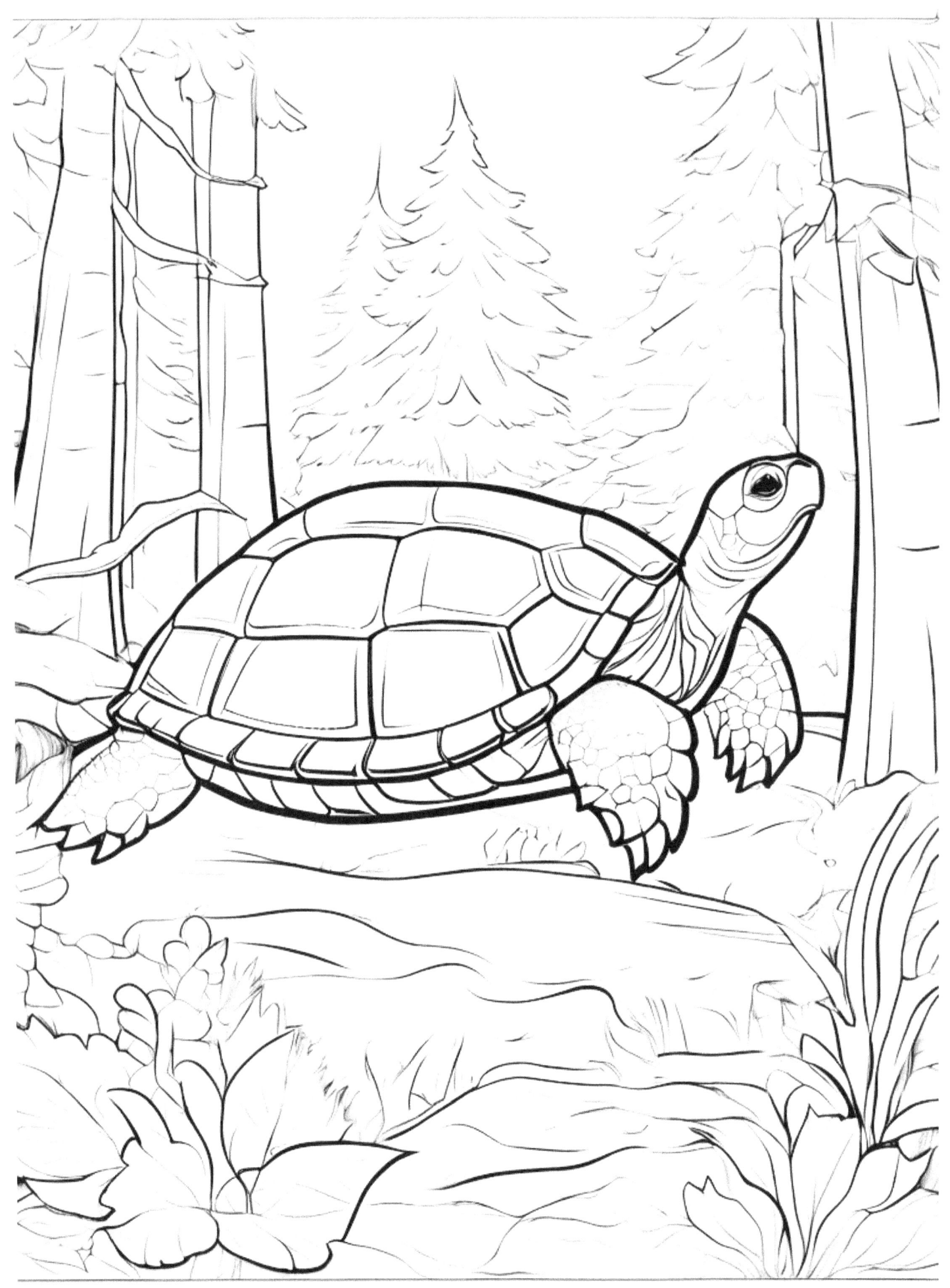

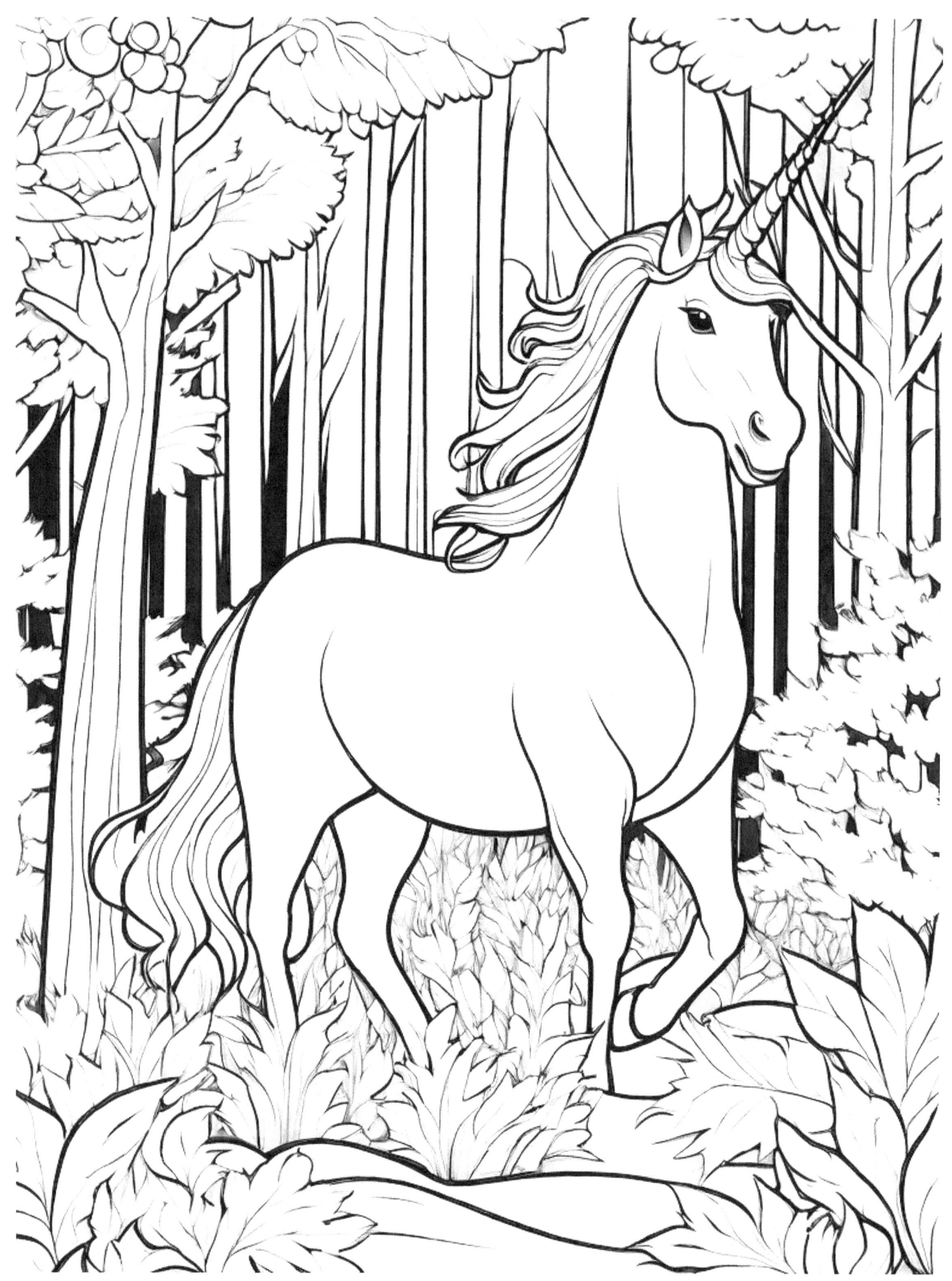

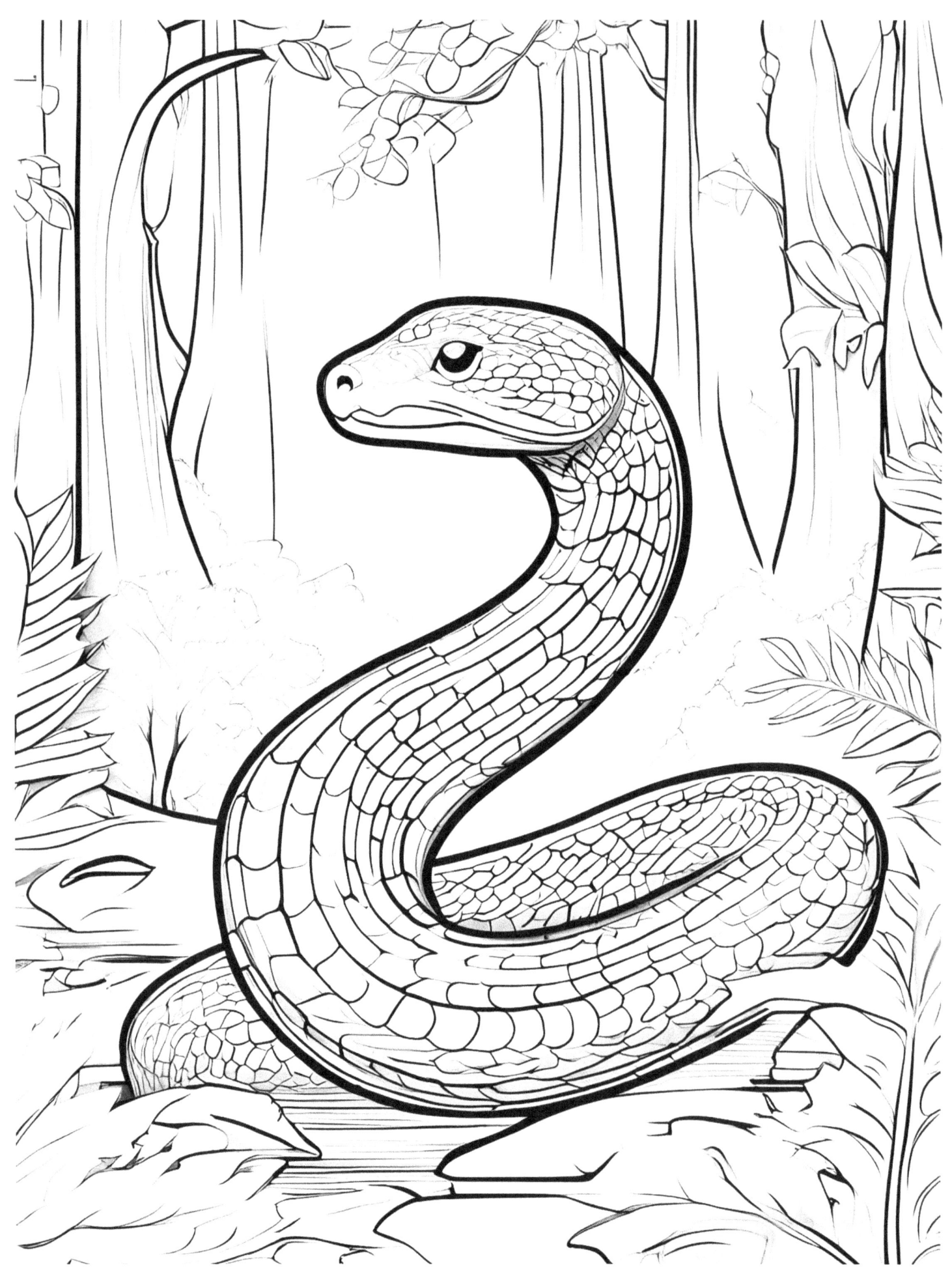

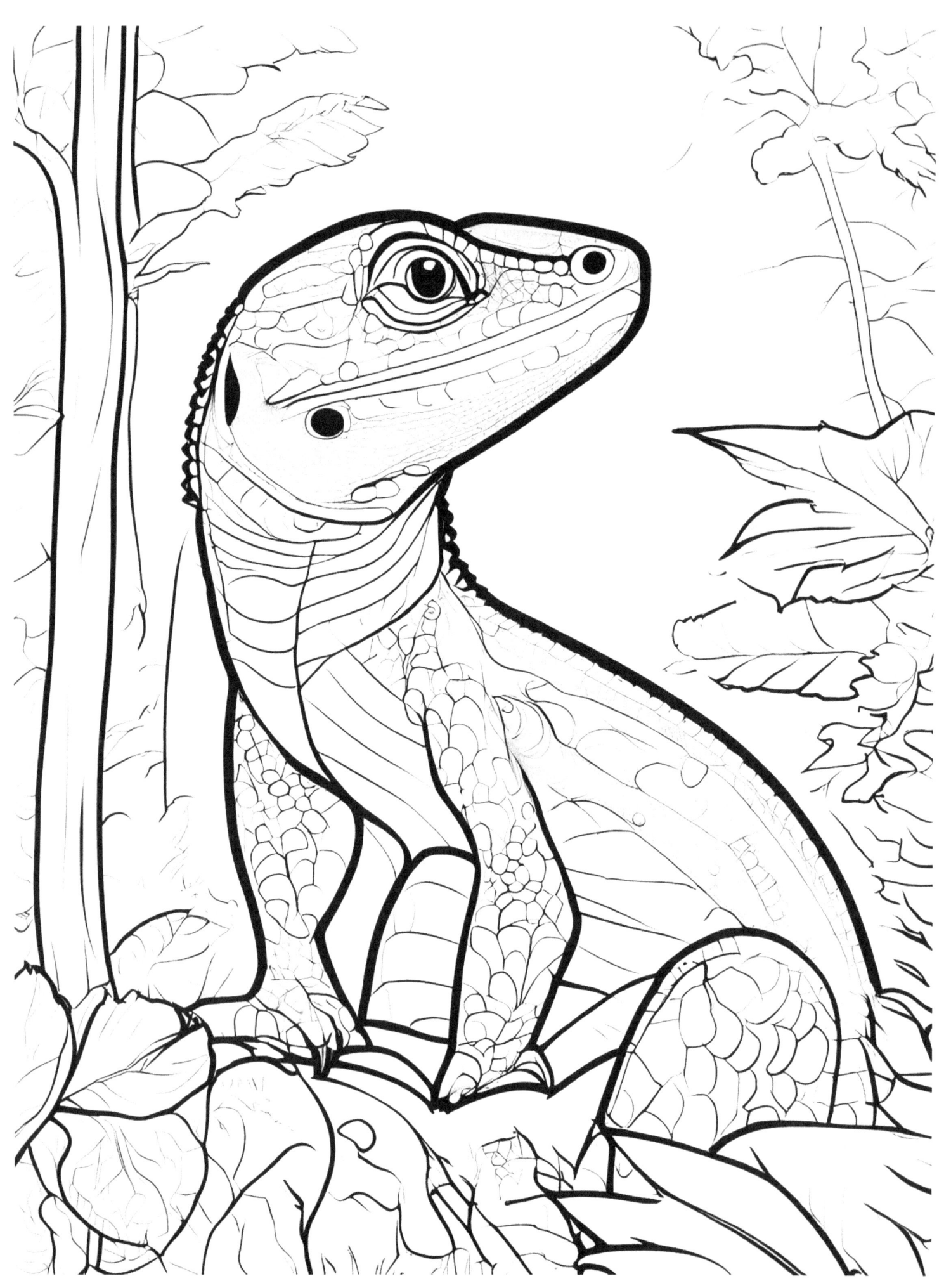

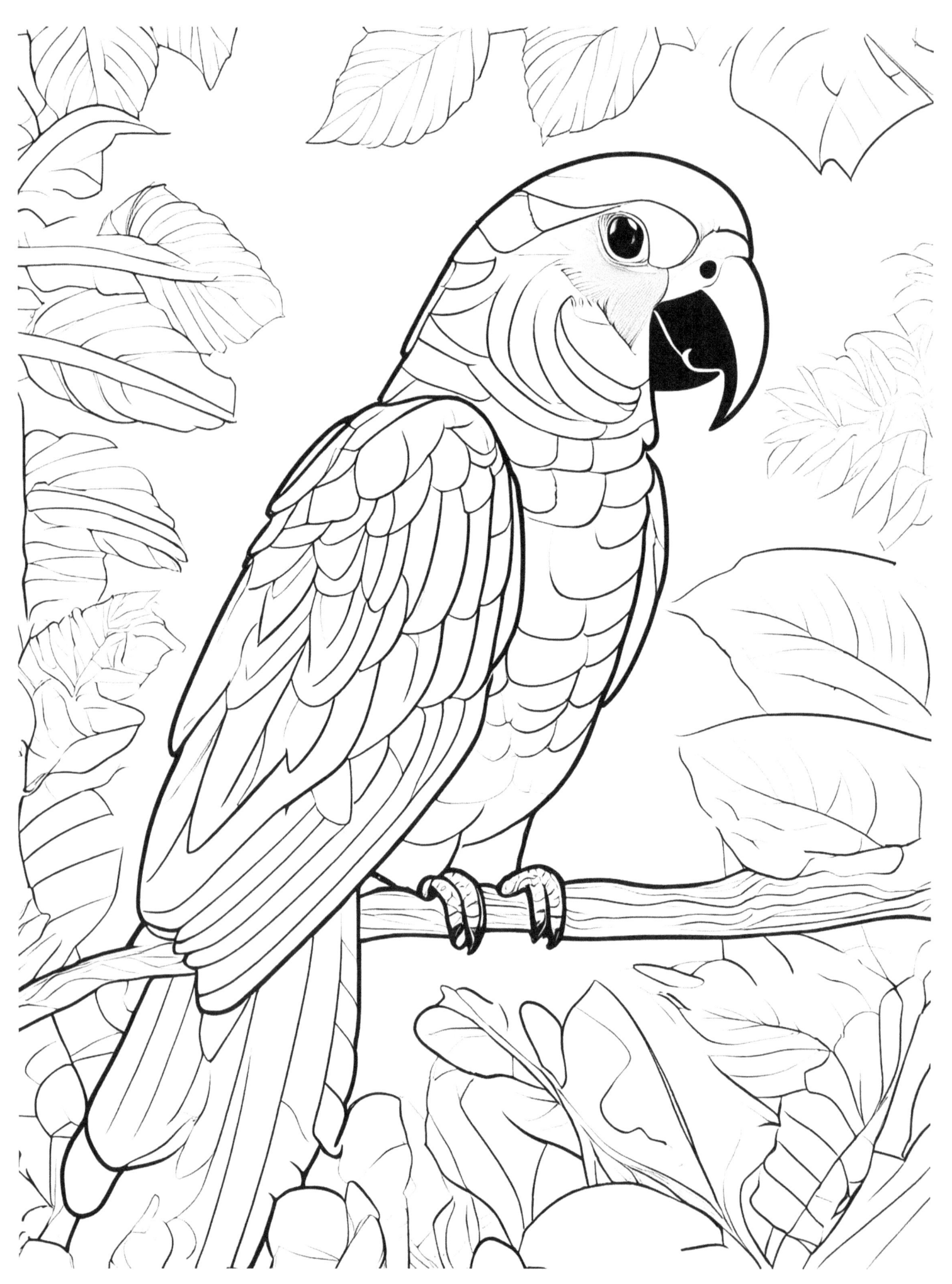

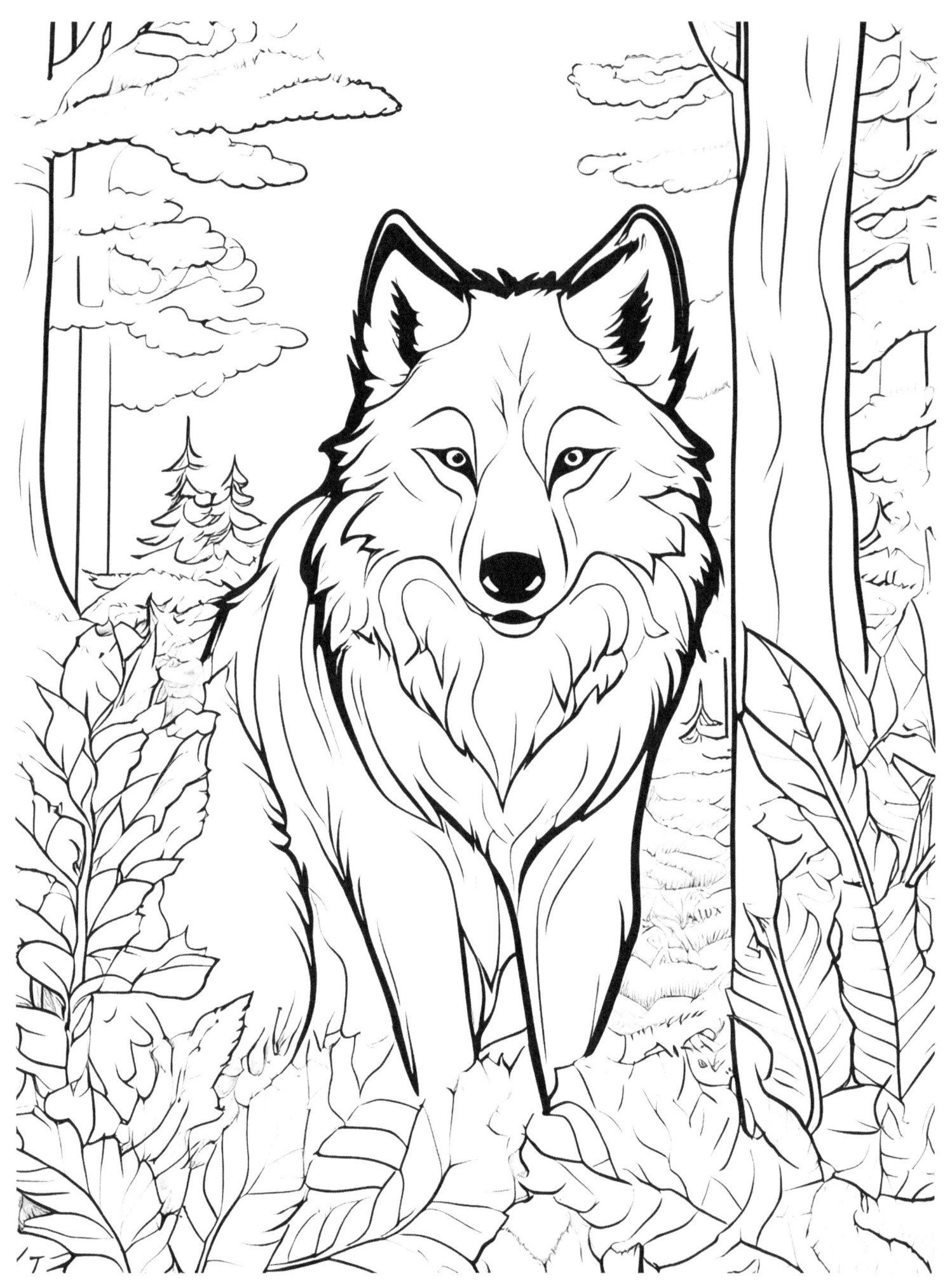

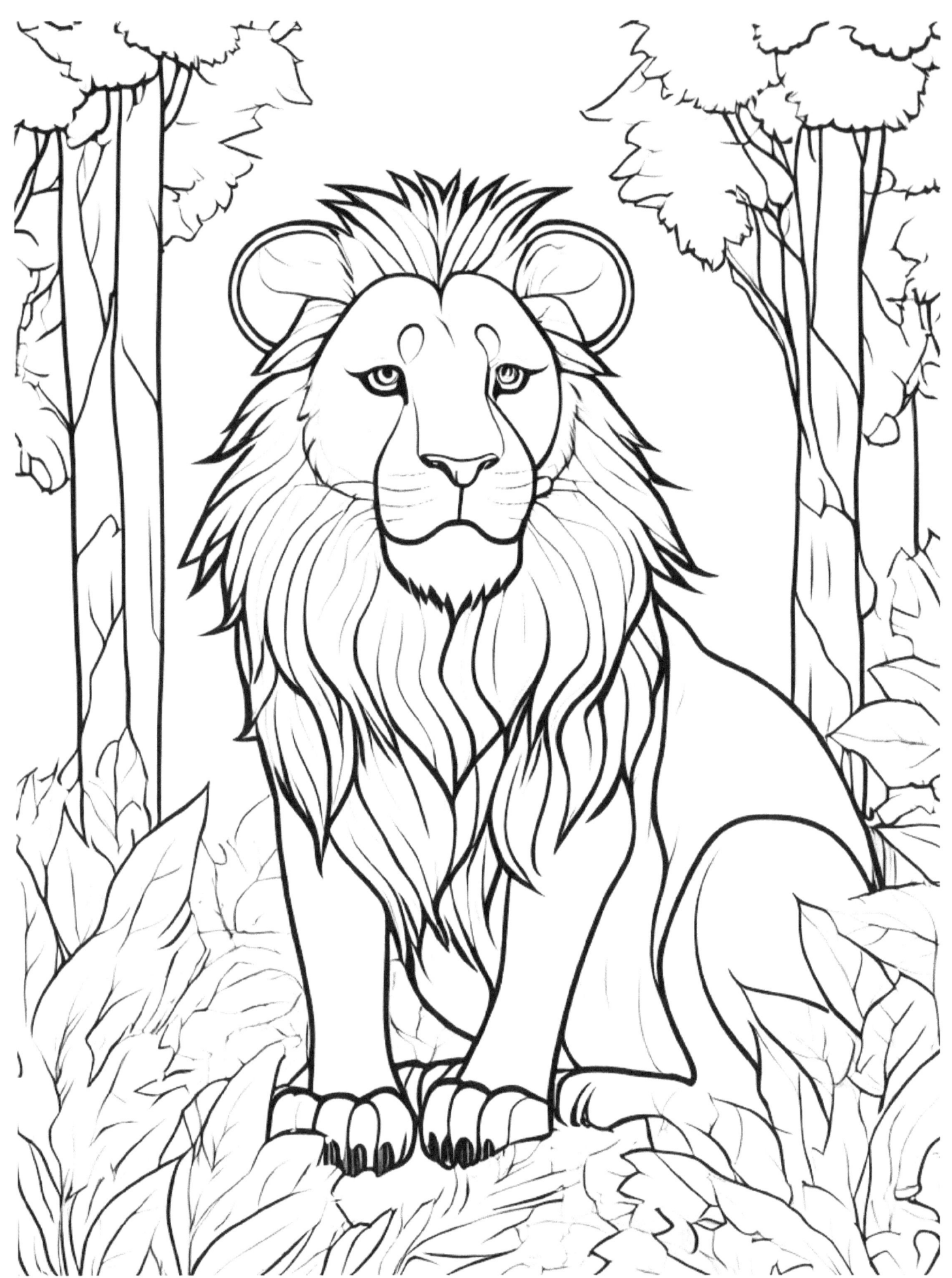

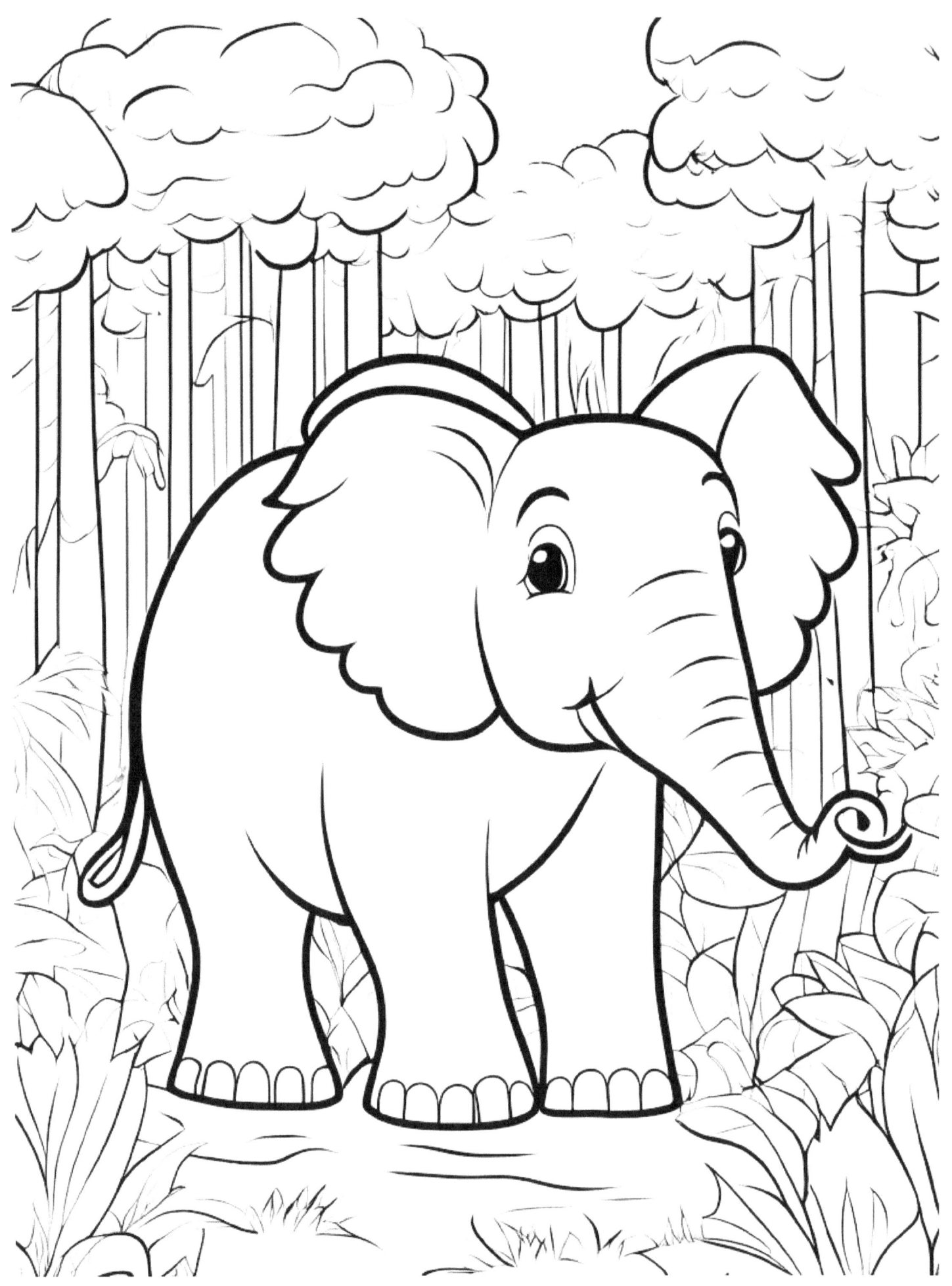

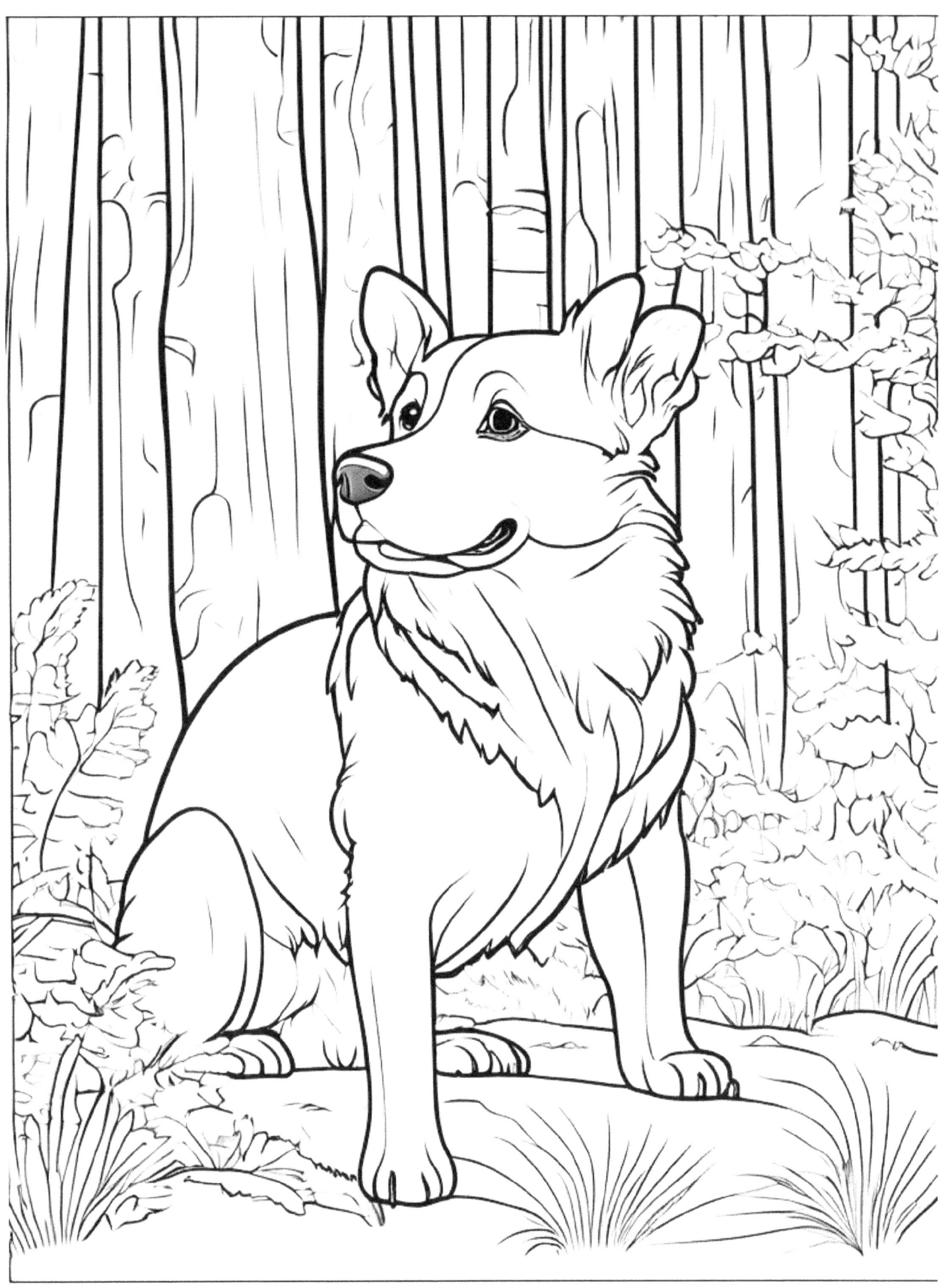

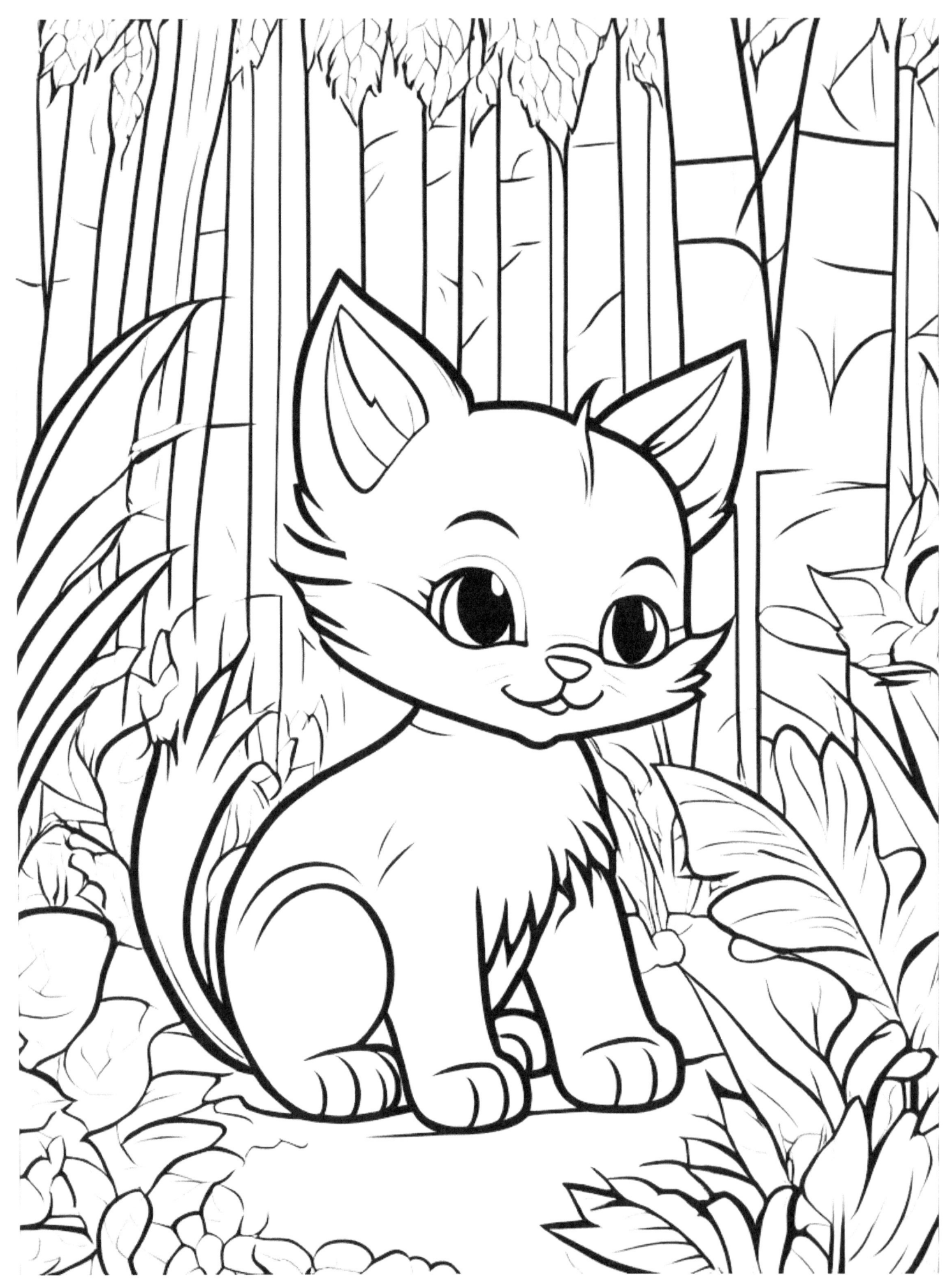

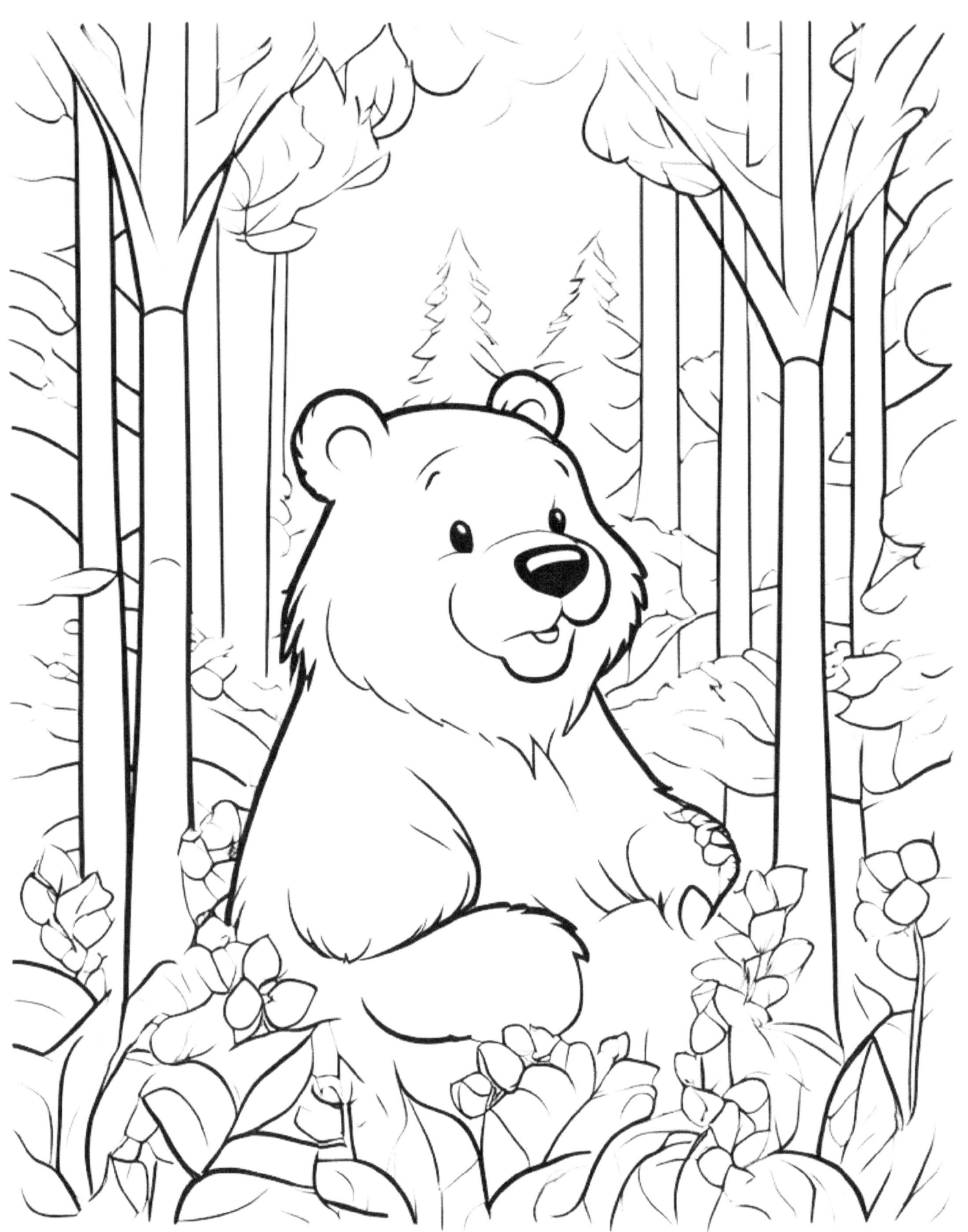

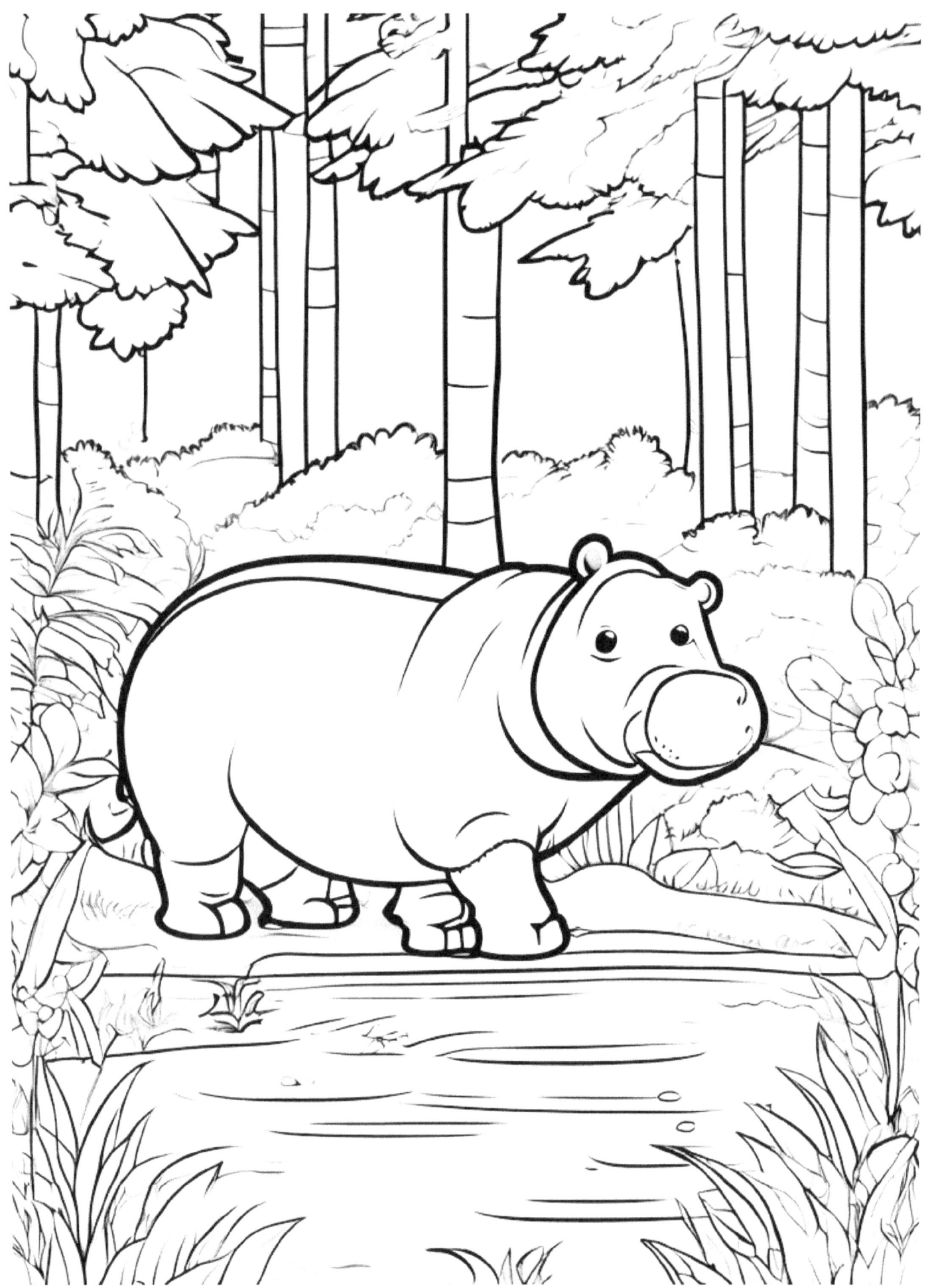

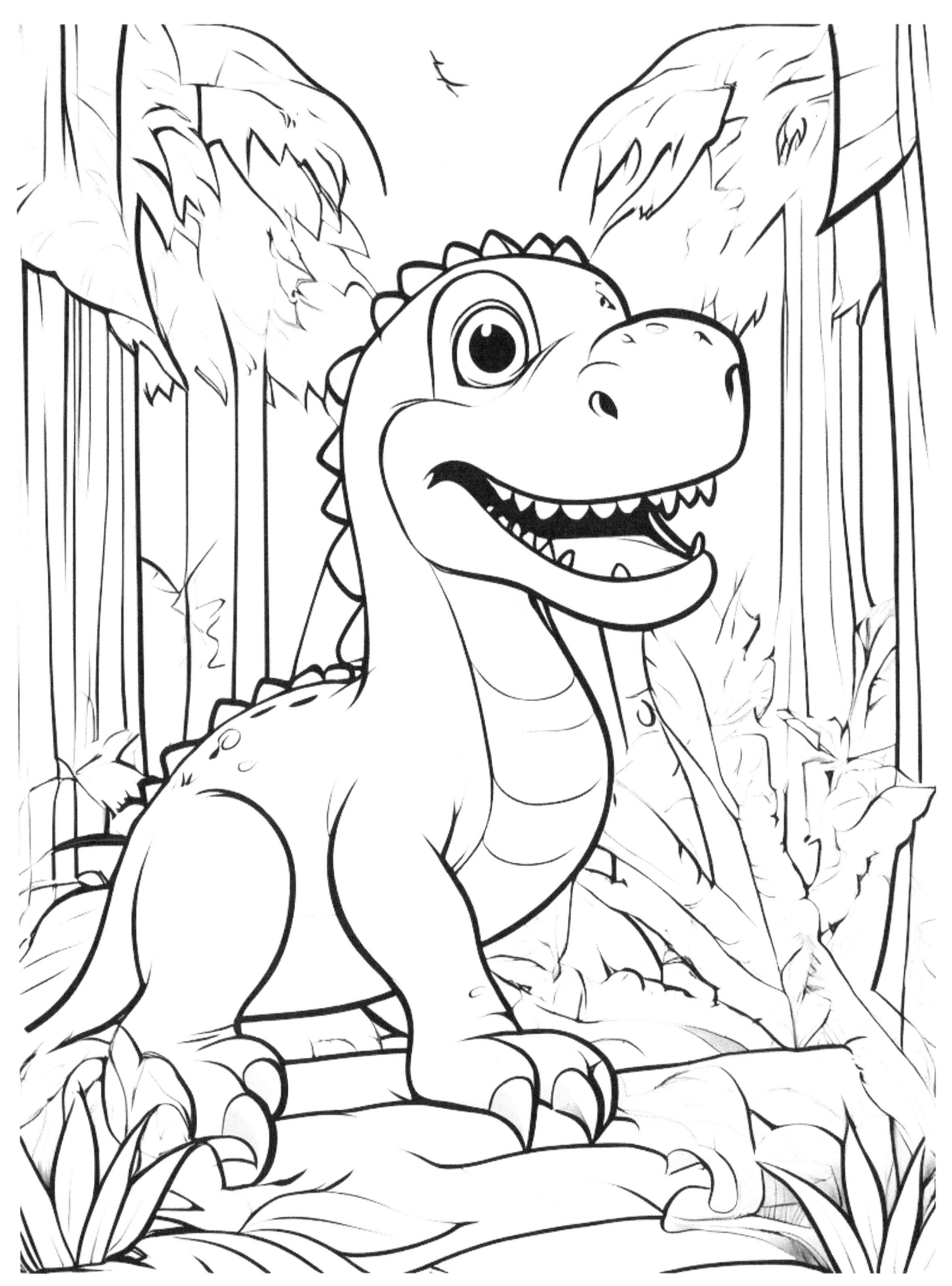

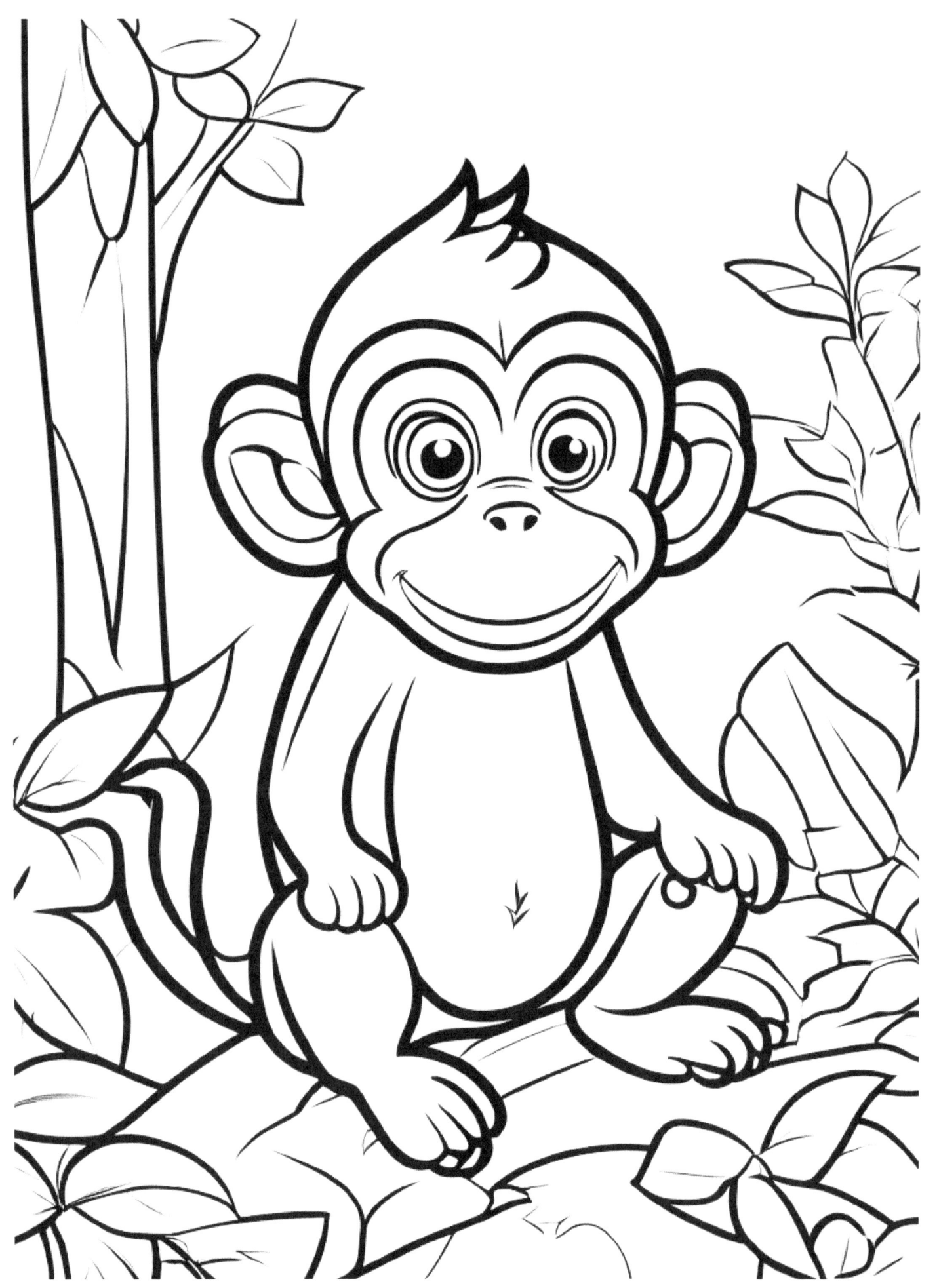

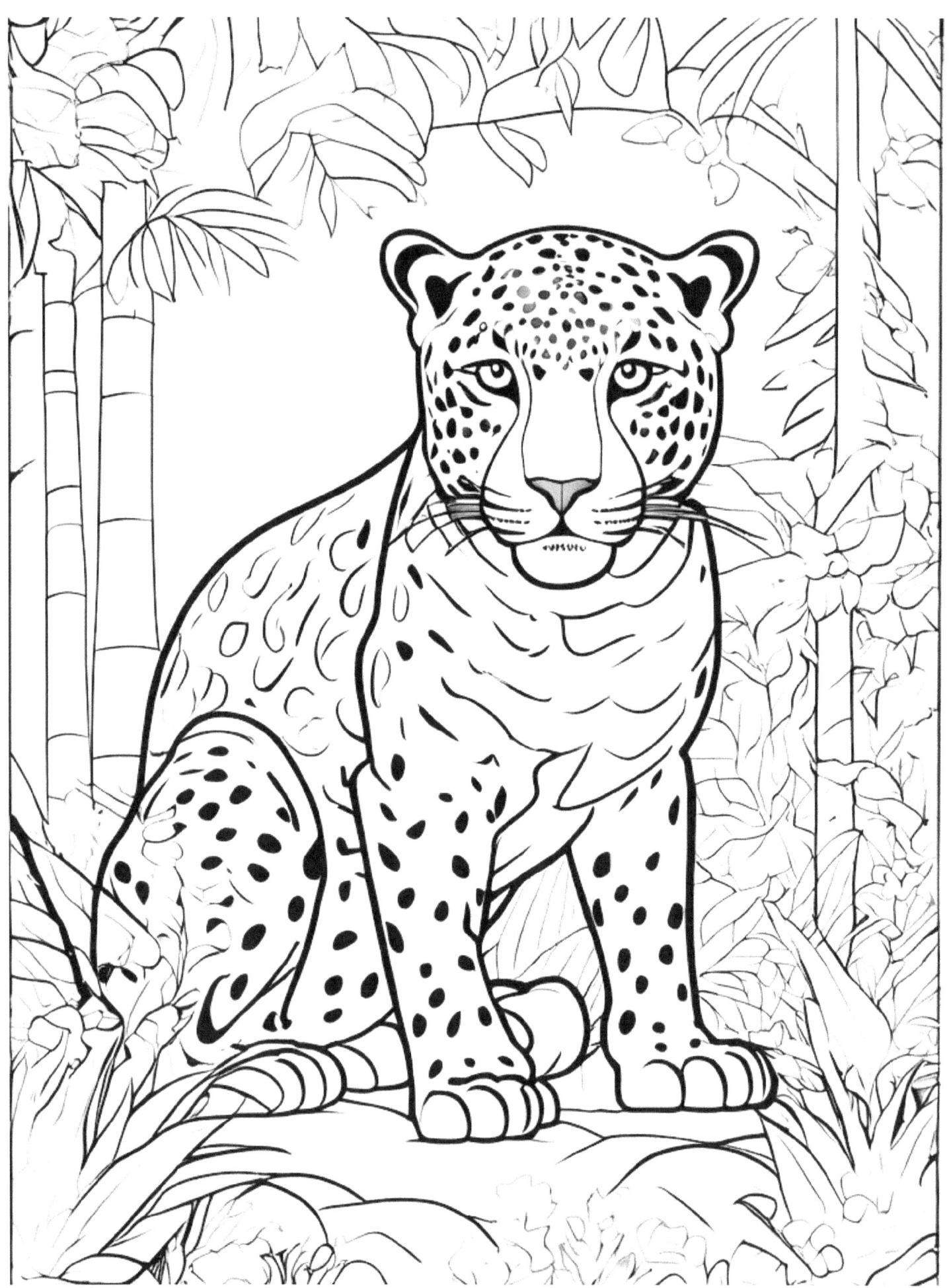

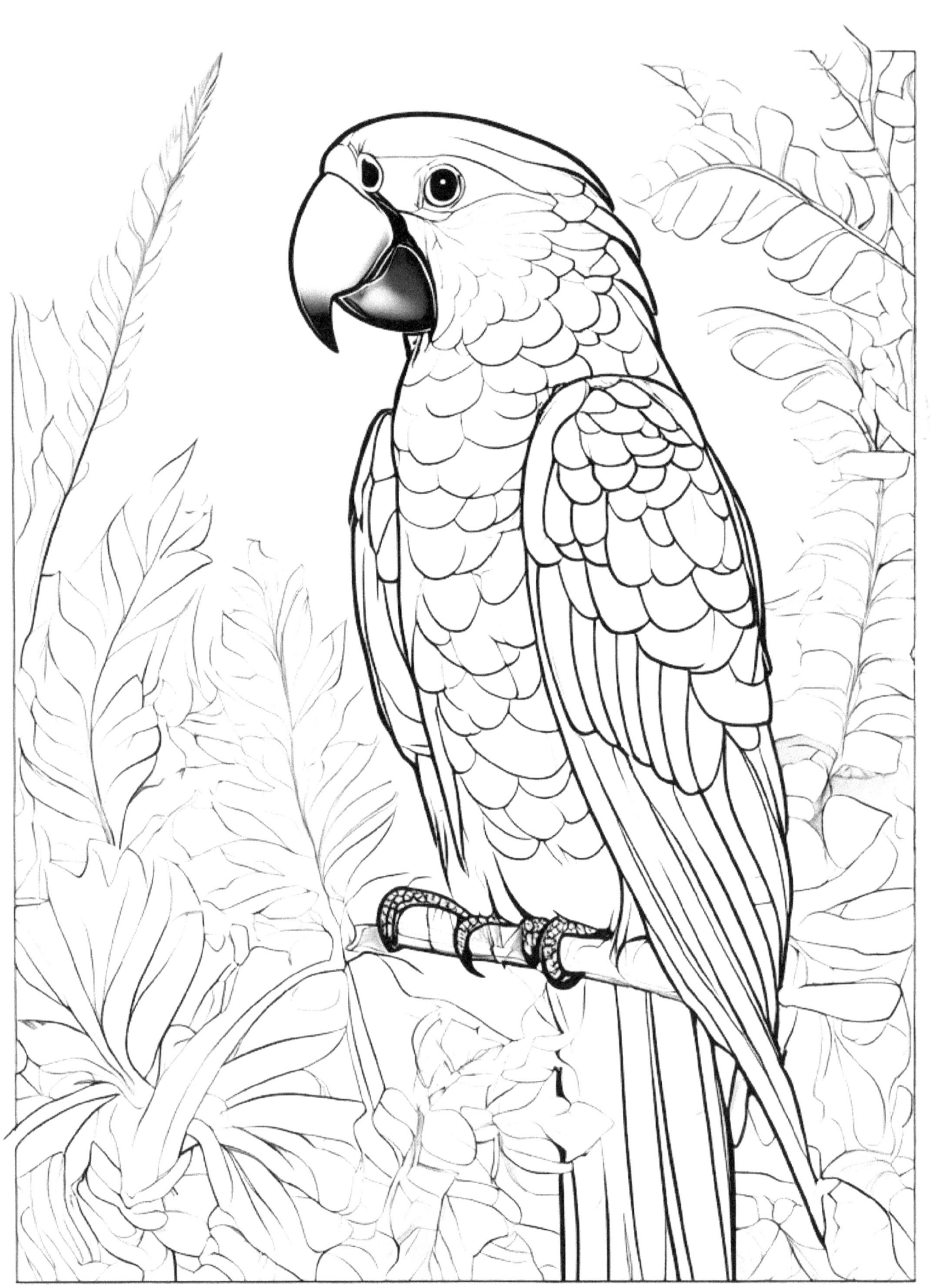

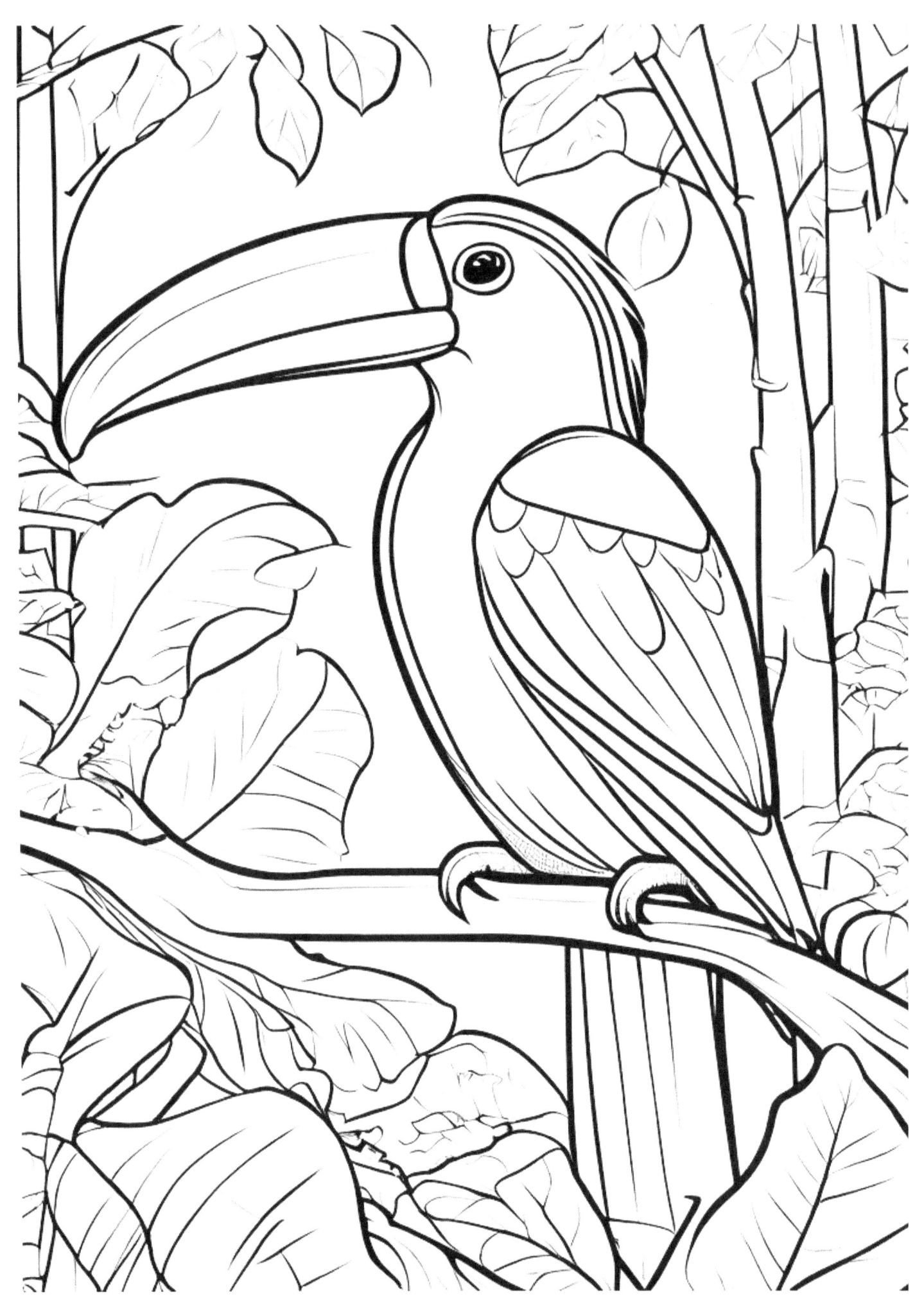

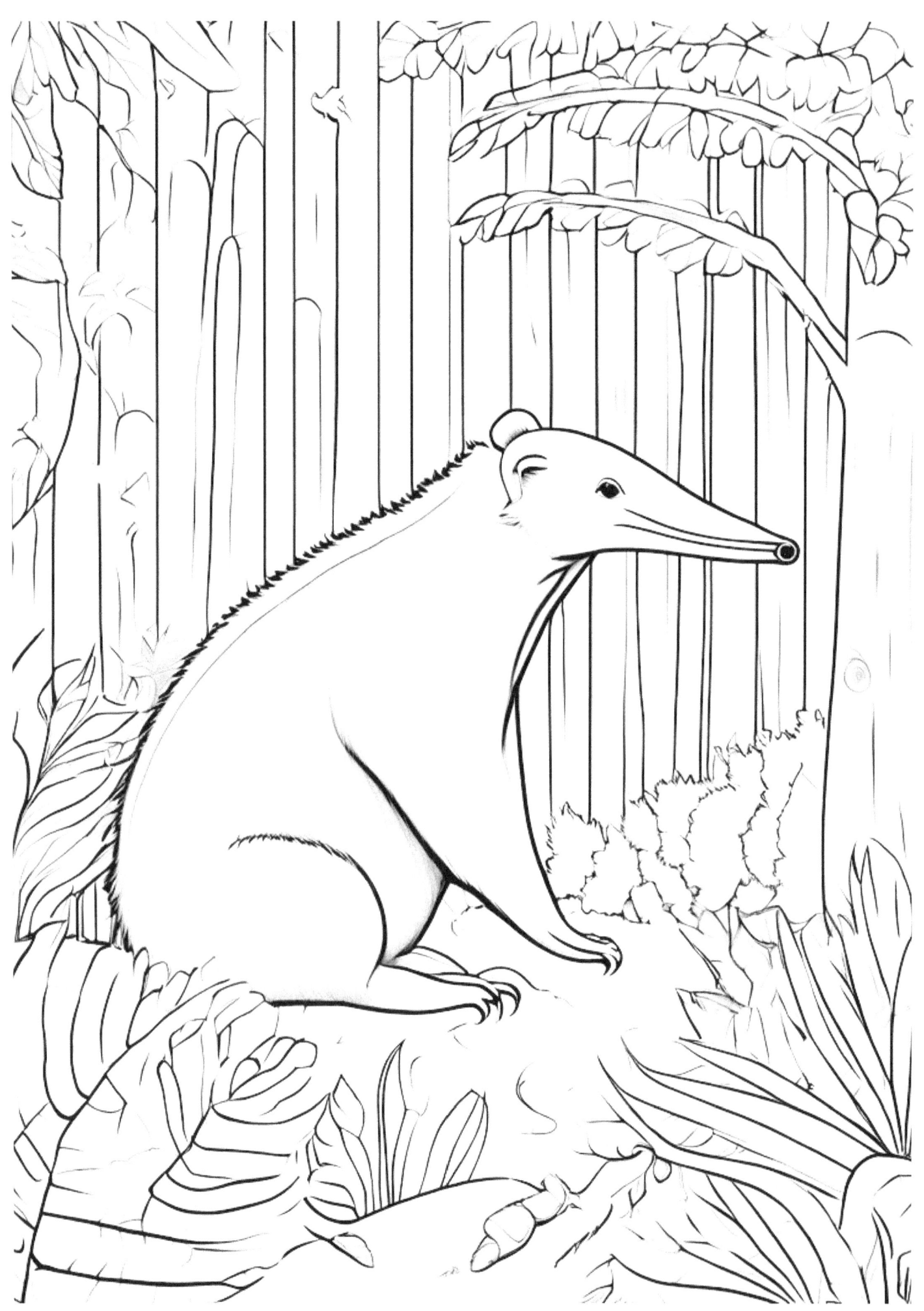

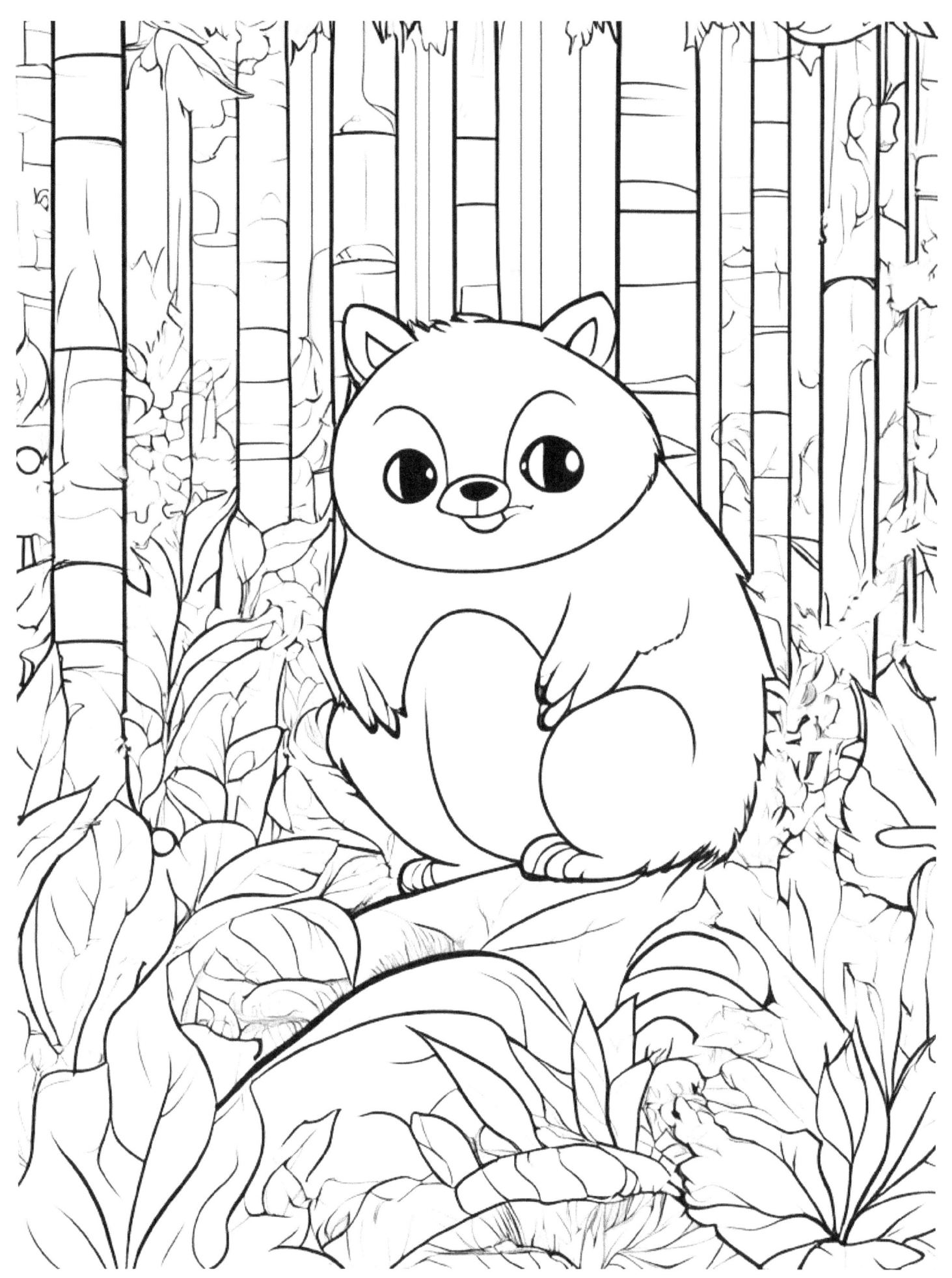

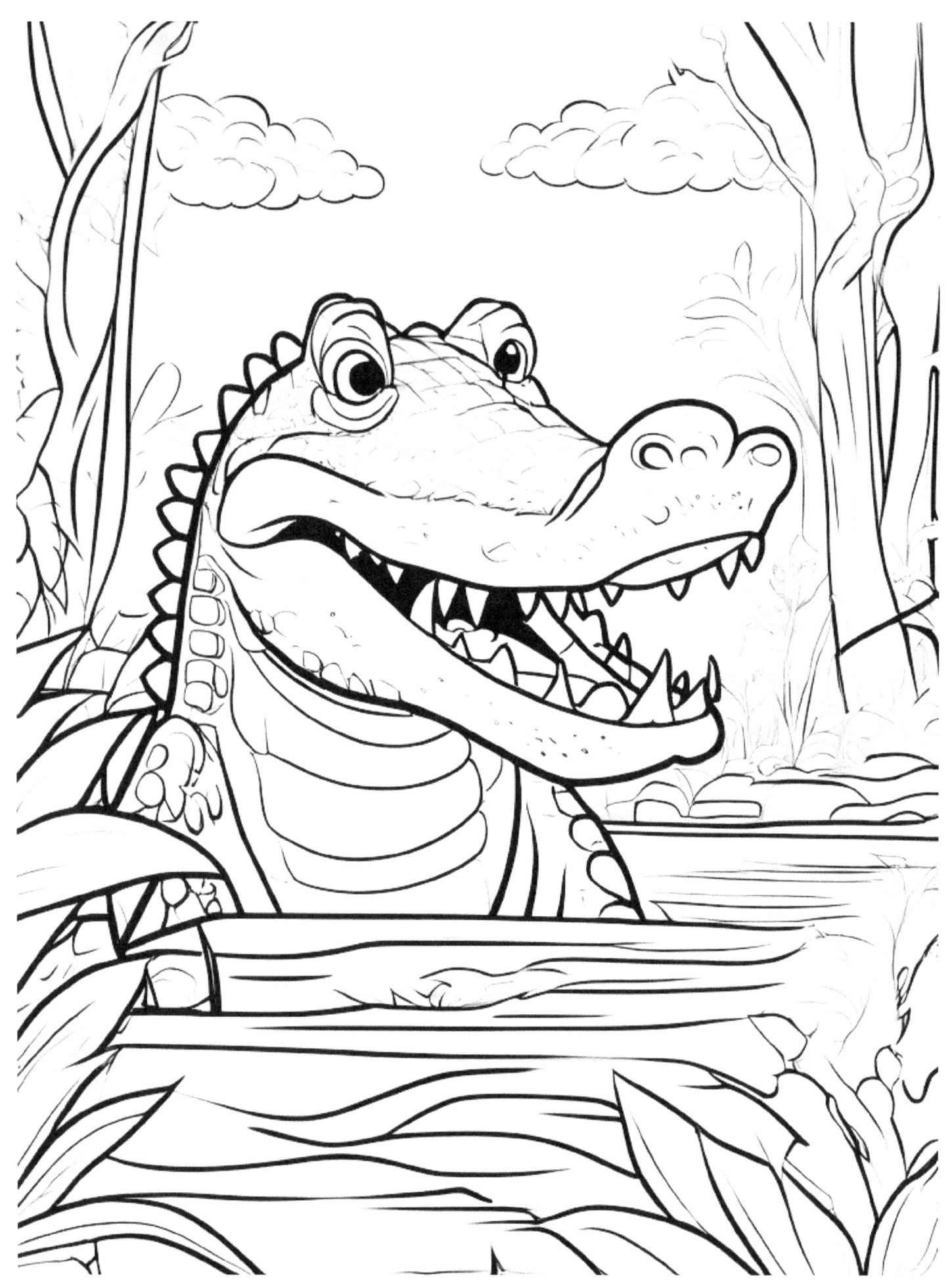

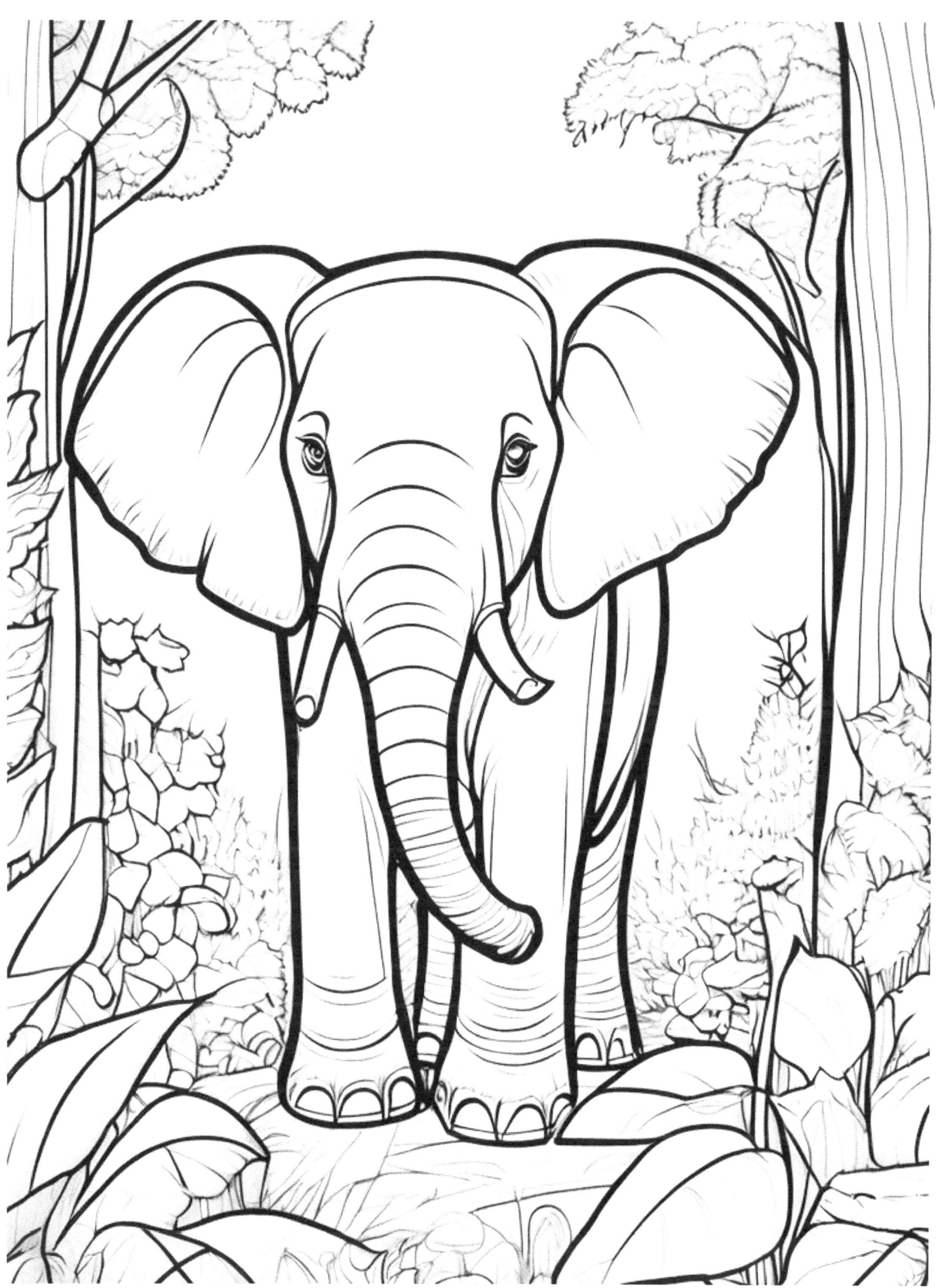

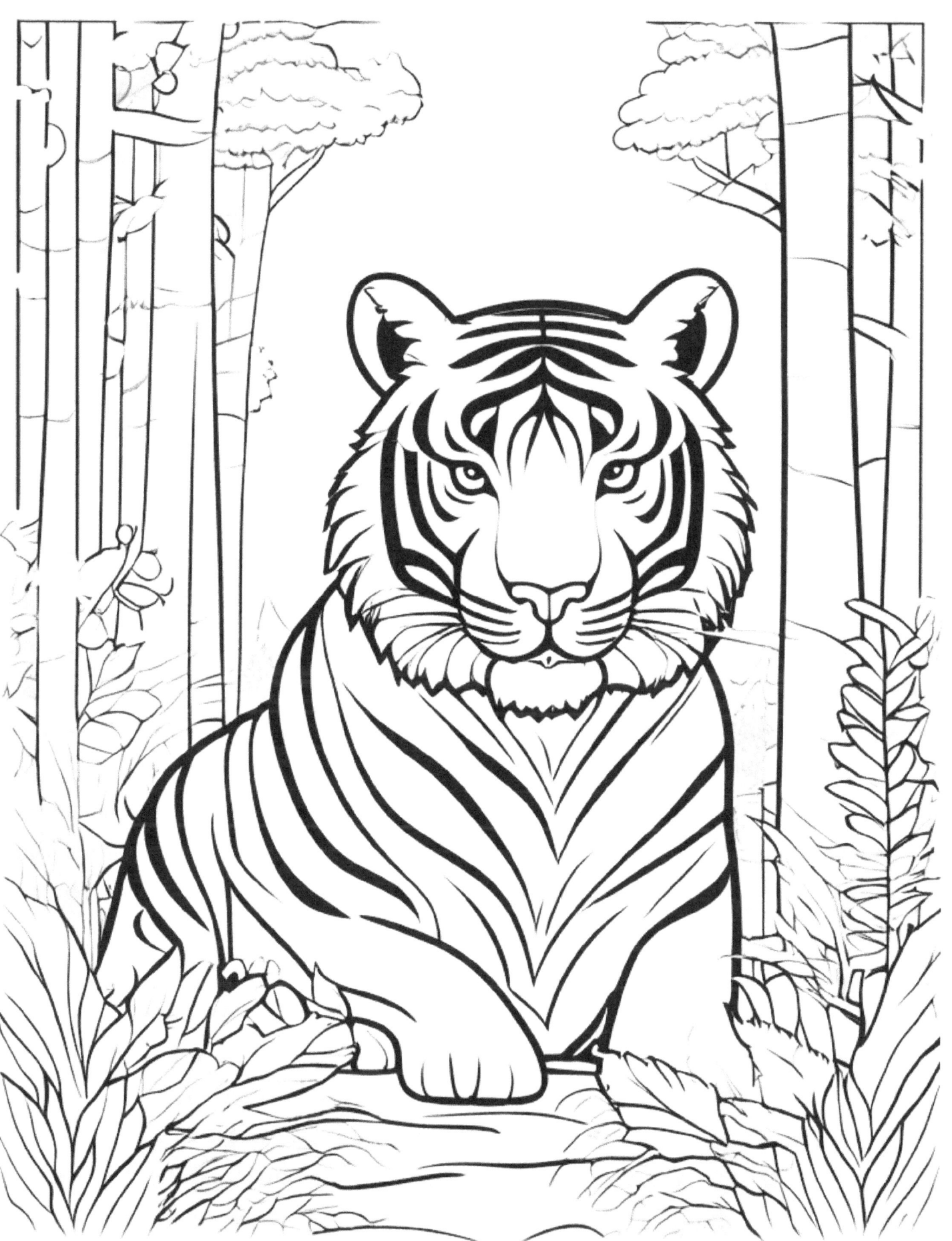

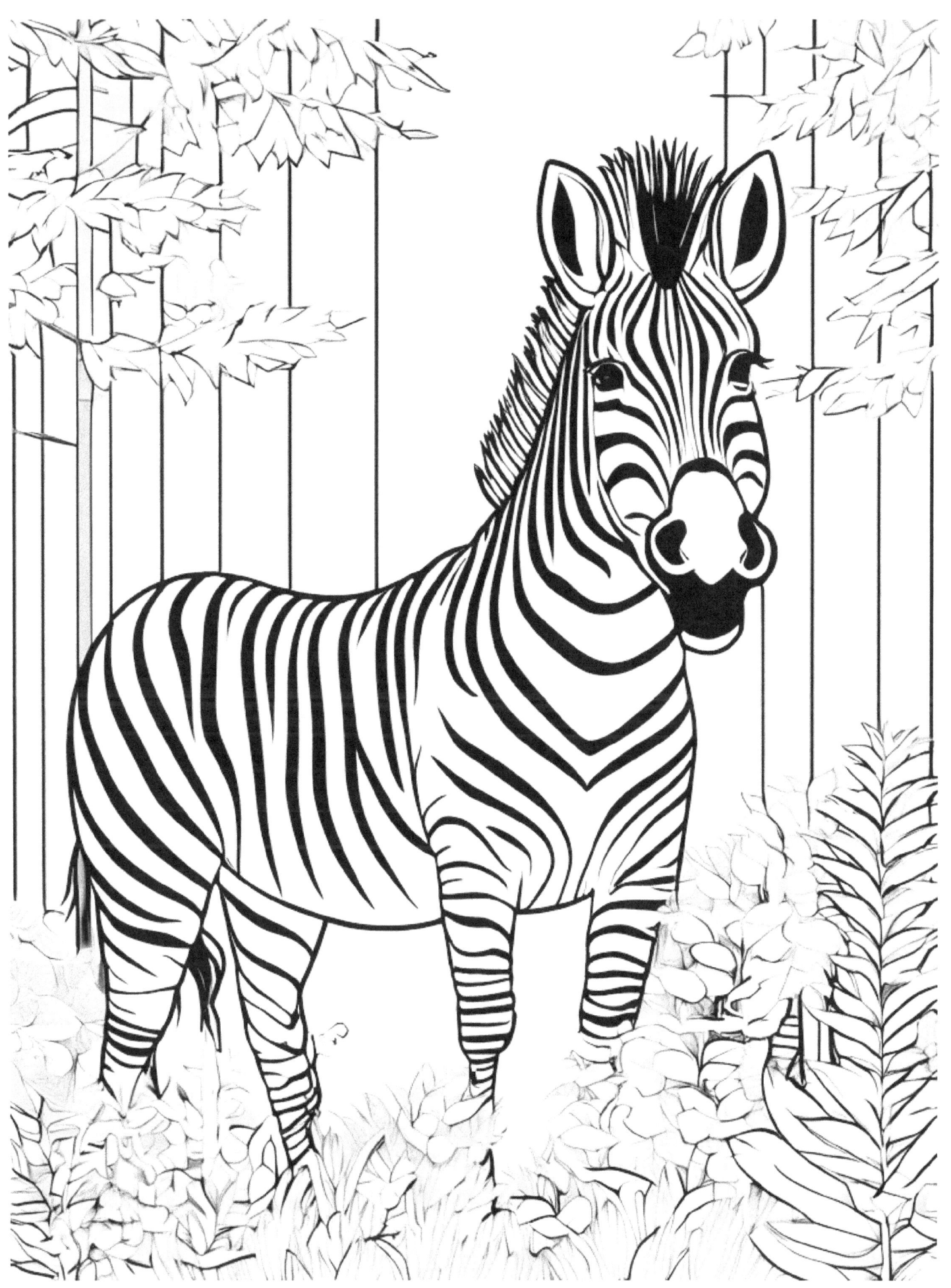

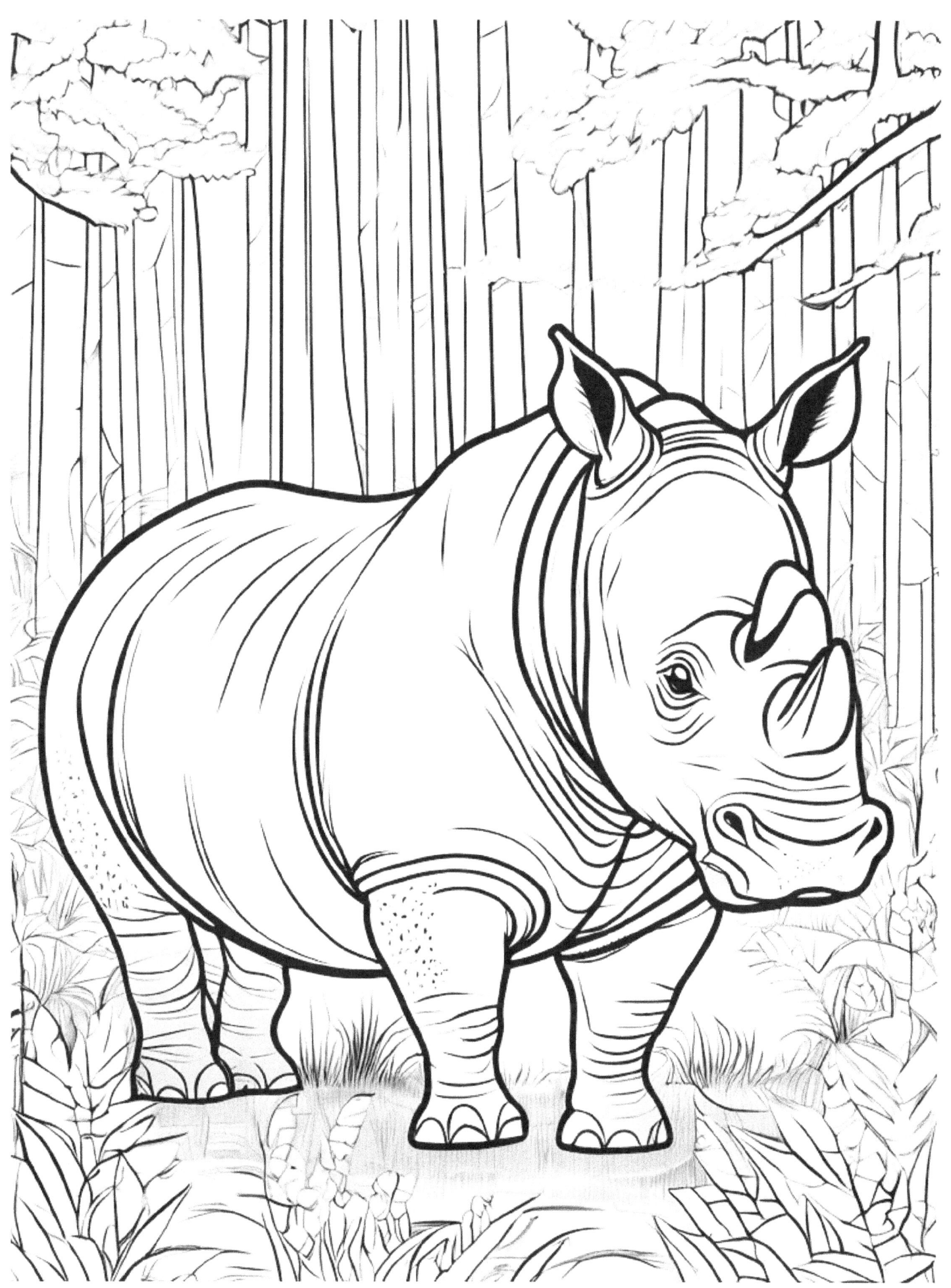

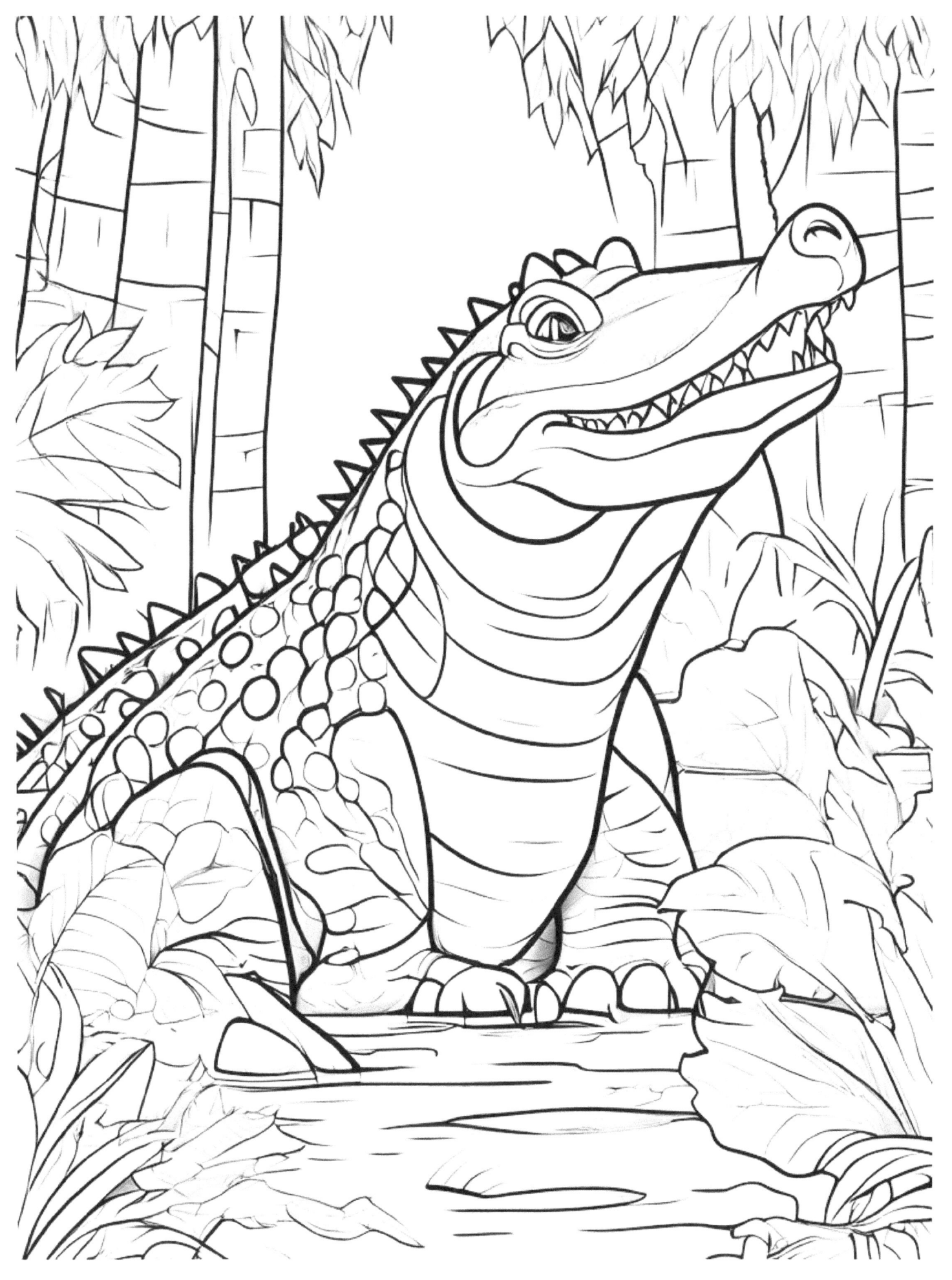

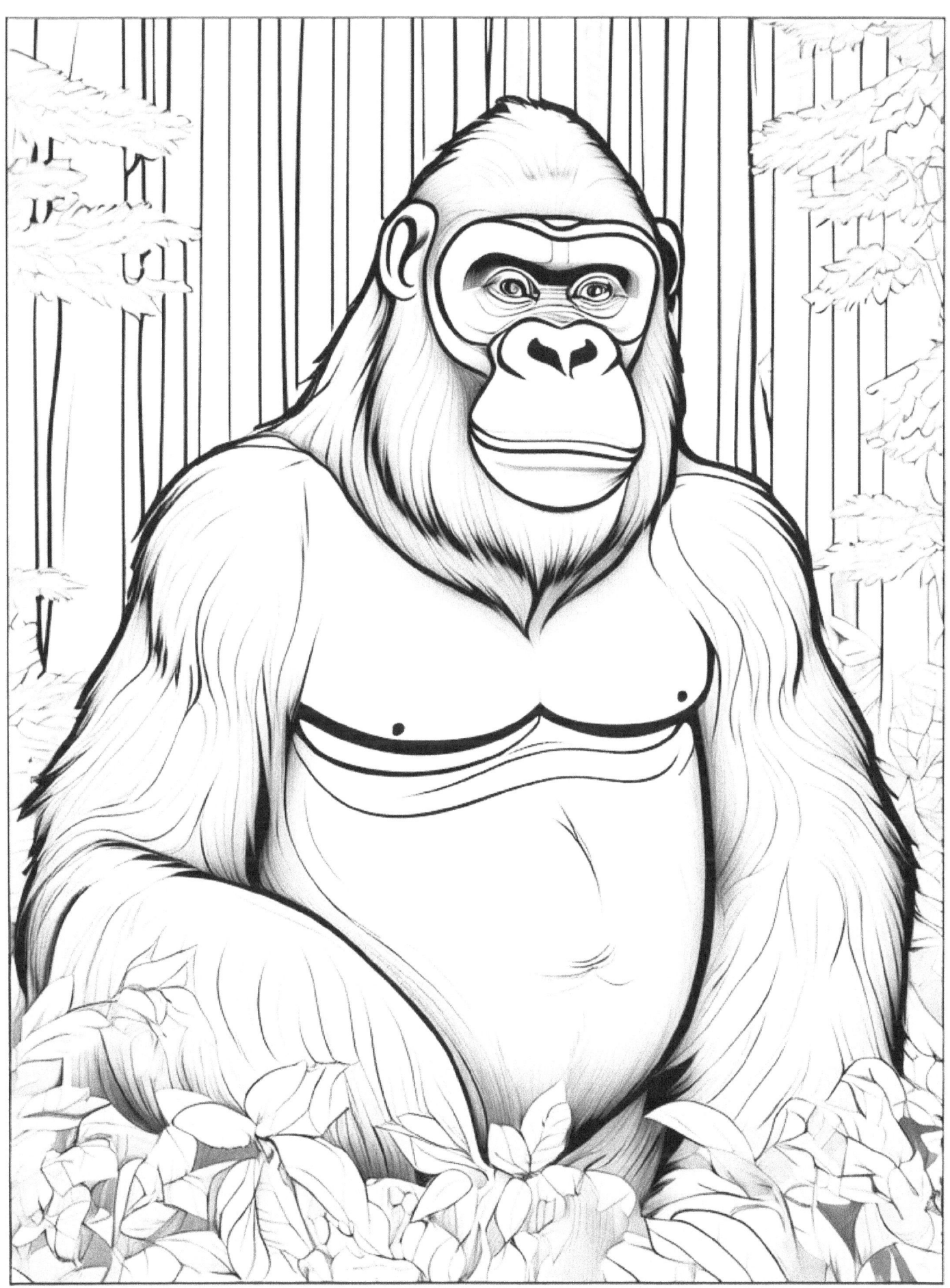

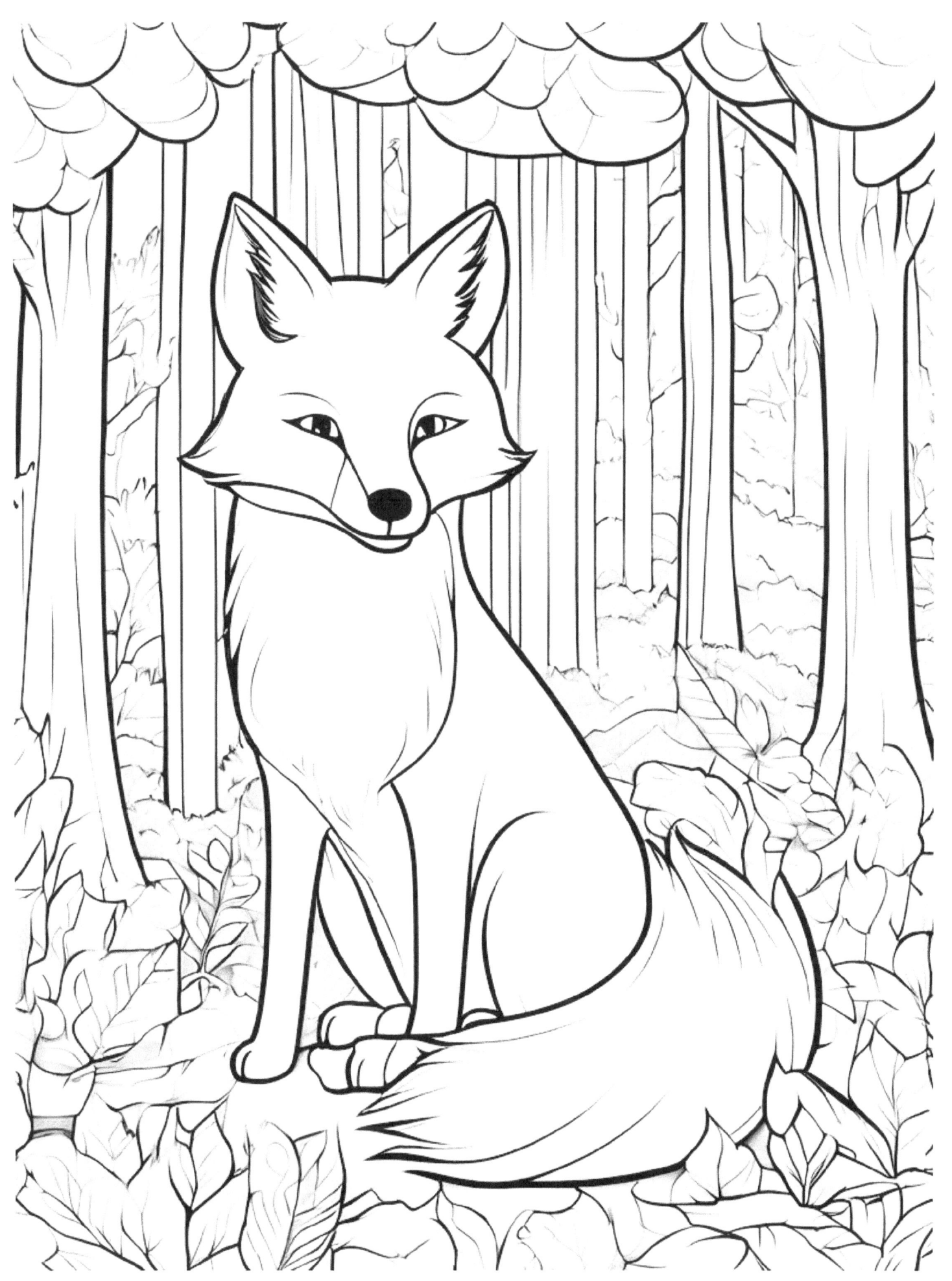

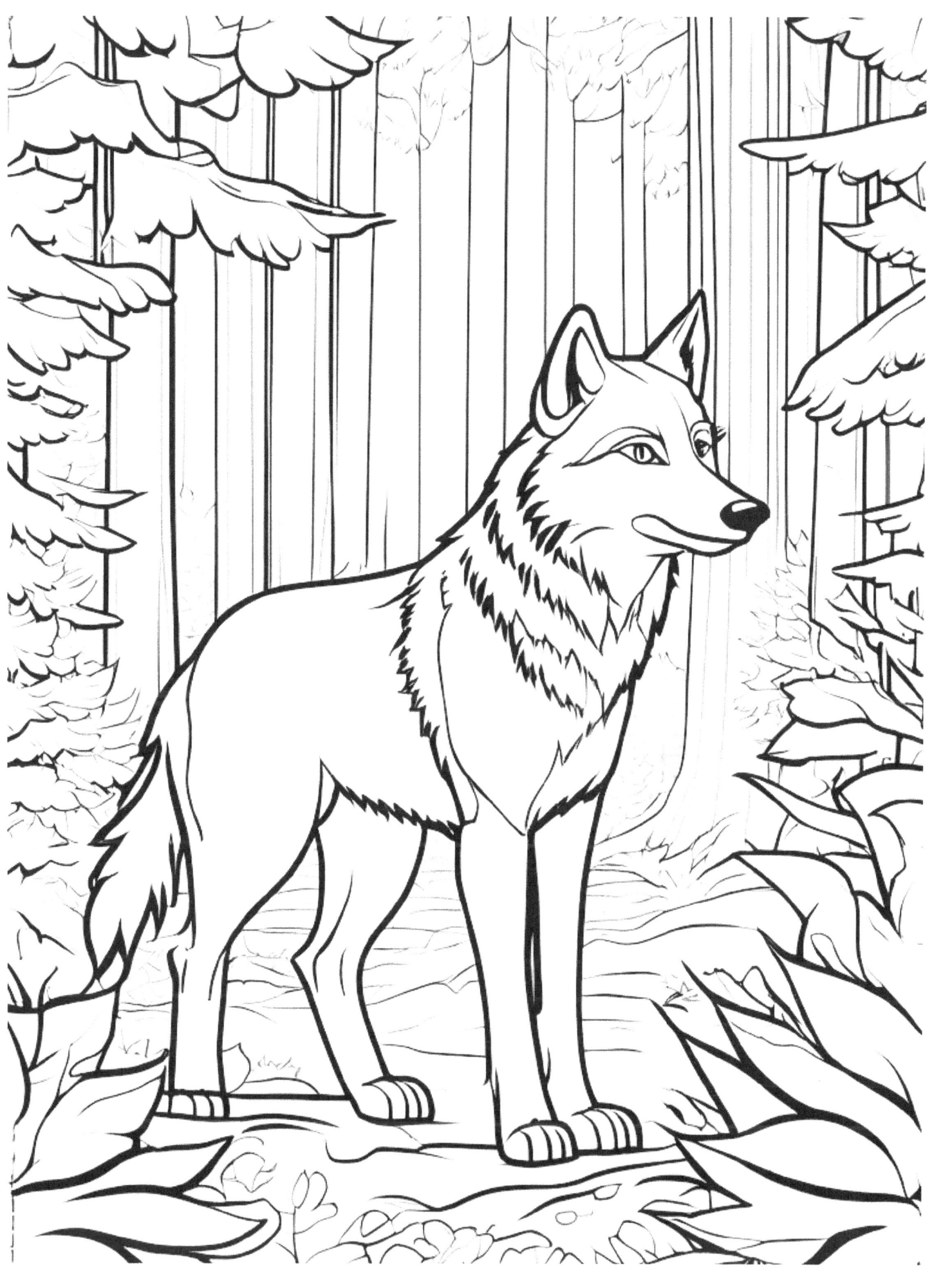

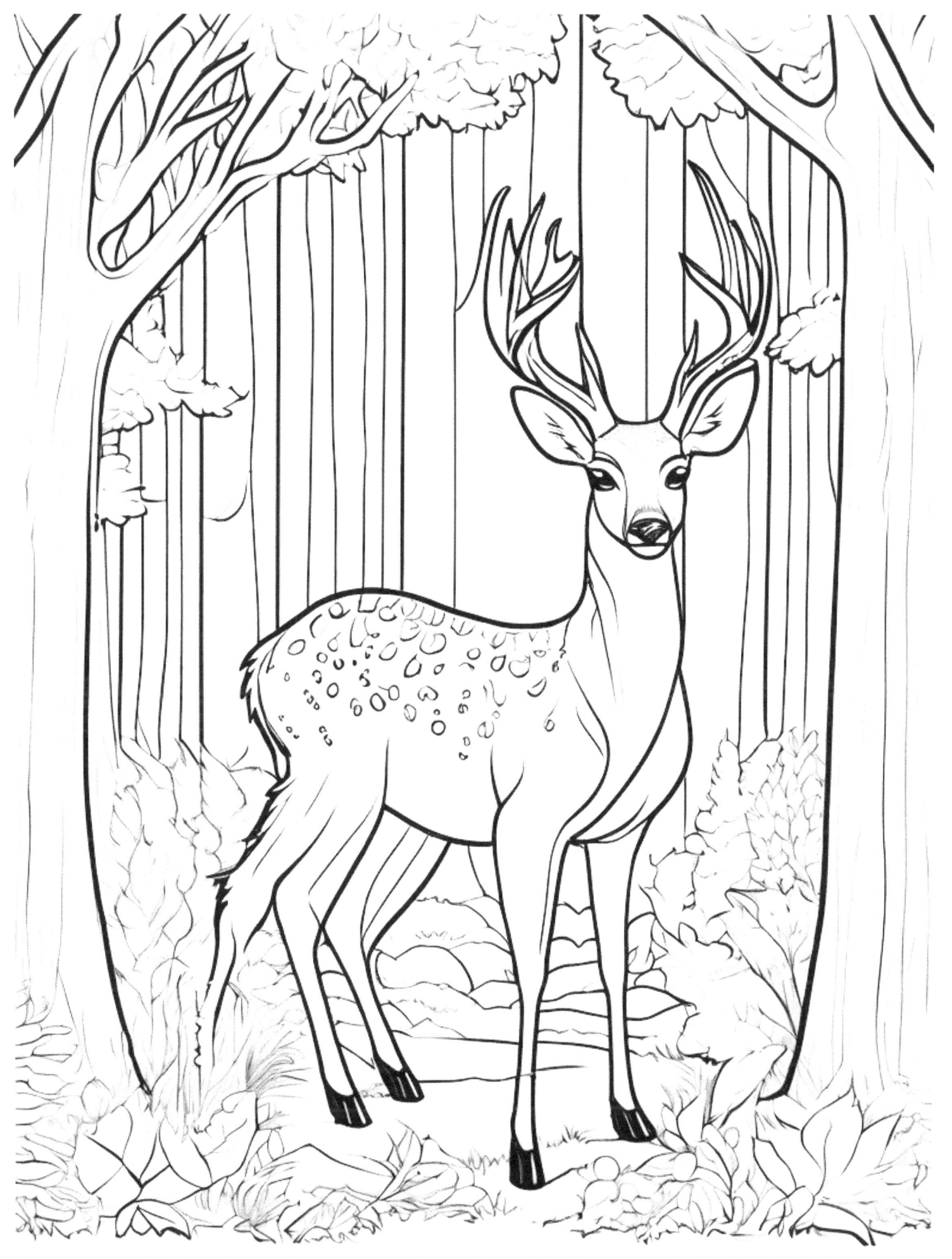

www.ingramcontent.com/pod-product-compliance
Lightning Source LLC
Chambersburg PA
CBHW080223220526
45470CB00015B/3082

Acknowledgments

I'd like to start by thanking God for giving me the strength and knowledge to do something I didn't think I was capable of doing.

Thank you to my husband and my children for supporting me and believing in me.

I thank my parents for their love and sacrifices. They sent me to a country away from them to get a better education. They continue to teach me about family values. I hope this will make them proud.

A special thanks to Sapphire who helped me throughout this crazy endeavor and by giving me ideas to make this book unique.

Thanks to Jennifer Kincade for finalizing the book for us to get it published!

Please enjoy this book,

Sangita Patel, Author

MY TONGUE NEEDS CLEANING, TOO!

Words to Know:

Dada: Grandfather

Dadi: Grandmother

Beta: an affectionate word for child

Ayurveda: a traditional Hindu system of medicine

Gulab Jamun: an Indian dessert that is round and soaked in a sweet syrup

Carrot Halwa: a sweet Indian pudding

Naan: a type of flat bread

Bacteria: tiny organisms that you cannot see with your eyes